Faith in Ulster

This book has received support from the Cultural Traditions Programme
of the Community Relations Council, which aims to encourage
acceptance and understanding of cultural diversity.

Published by:
Evangelical Contribution On Northern Ireland
12 Wellington Place, Belfast BT1 6GE

Design by: Spring Graphics
Printed & Bound by: GPS Colour Graphics Limited
© ECONI 1996   ISBN 1 874324 01 8

Faith in Ulster

edited by Alwyn Thomson
Research Officer: Evangelical Contribution On Northern Ireland

Contents

Foreword David Porter   6

Introduction Alwyn Thomson   8

John Alderdice   14

Arthur Aughey   16

Glen Barr   18

Geoffrey Beattie   21

Eileen Bell   23

Esmond Birnie   25

28   David Bleakley

30   Ken Bloomfield

32   Myrtle Boal

34   Gareth Burke

36   Gregory Campbell

38   Fred Catherwood

40   George Crory

42   Tony Crowe

45   John Dickinson

47   Edward Donnelly

49   Robin Eames

				96	John Robb
				98	Patrick Roche
				101	John Ross
				103	Pearl Sagar
Brian Ervine	51	Michael Longley	74	105	Martin Smyth
Roy Garland	53	Gordon Lucy	76	107	Roz Stirling
Will Glendinning	55	Roy Magee	78	109	Steve Stockman
Ken Groves	57	Ian Major	80	111	Mervyn Storey
Michael Hall	59	Billy Malcolmson	82	113	William Temple
David Hewitt	61	David McConaghie	84	115	Chris Walpole
Finlay Holmes	64	Billy Mitchell	86	117	Stephen Williams
Mark Houston	66	James Molyneaux	88	119	Chris Wright
David Jardine	68	Philip Orr	90		
Brian Kennaway	70	Norman Porter	92		
Billy Kennedy	72	Paul Reid	94		

Foreword

IN NOVEMBER 1985 THE BRITISH PRIME MINISTER, MARGARET THATCHER, AND THE Irish *taoiseach,* Garret Fitzgerald, signed the Anglo-Irish Agreement marking a new phase in Anglo-Irish relations. For many in the unionist community it was an act of betrayal. Not for the first time they perceived a threat to their political and cultural identity. That this identity was bound up with their religion - Protestantism - was evident in the wave of protest that followed.

Sermons were preached, prayers offered and Ulster's battle hymn, *O God Our Help in Ages Past,* resounded at rallies throughout the province. The religious language and metaphor utilised in the political discourse of unionism was not new, nor was this the last occasion on which it was to be applied. While Northern Ireland cannot be understood solely in terms of a religious conflict, the potent mix of religion and national identity brings a dimension to our politics and, more significantly, to the witness of Christians which cannot be ignored.

It was against this background that an advertisement appeared in the Belfast Telegraph in November 1985. Signed by 24 Presbyterian ministers, it was headed *For God and His Glory Alone* - a phrase reflecting that other phrase with its particular resonance in the Protestant community. In September 1988, this heading became the title of a booklet. Signed by 200 evangelical leaders from across the Protestant denominations, it highlighted ten biblical principles and challenged evangelical Protestants to reassess their role in the divided community of Northern Ireland.

From this publication emerged ECONI - Evangelical Contribution On Northern Ireland. ECONI asked questions: Had evangelicals in our community failed a test of loyalty? Had we been guilty of setting aside the values and priorities of the Kingdom of God in the cause of defending Ulster? Had Ulster - the land, the culture, the Protestant people - become our God? For Ulster evangelicals in the choice between Faith and Ulster, was it God who had lost out?

Since then much of ECONI's work has focused on these questions. In asking and addressing them we have sought to listen to God - studying the Bible and applying biblical principles to our life and witness in a divided community.

Yet the zeal of the new convert can lead to a neglect of the obvious. In a desire to distance oneself from a rejected ideology, it is all too easy to distance oneself from those for whom it still has meaning. In the rush to speak, to be an alternative voice, there is the danger that we no longer listen to the legitimate hopes and fears, hurts and expectations of those with whom we differ.

This collection is an exercise in listening. It arises from our reflections on religious nationalism and our recognition that, like many in Ulster, we, too, have failed to listen: to those who share our evangelical Protestant faith but reach different conclusions concerning their relationship to Ulster; to those who do not share that faith but have other, different, perspectives - political and cultural - to bring.

Jesus often began his discourses with a question - an invitation to others to say what was on their mind, an opportunity to listen.

Introduction

A Question of Identity

IT IS A COMMONPLACE TO DECLARE THAT THE UNIONIST PEOPLE OF NORTHERN Ireland are unsure of their identity. Are they of Britain? Ireland? Ulster? How should they relate to an Irish state that claims to want them but which they perceive as hostile and different? How should they relate to a British state that they look to but which they perceive as cynical and indifferent?

Yet perhaps even to speak of 'the unionist people', as though there were a single coherent group of men and women who could be described and discussed collectively, is already assuming too much.

The existence of so many parties and organisations with that significant U in the name is only the most obvious indication of the diverse nature of unionism. Of course, there is the other U - Ulster - appearing in the names of other parties and organisations, suggesting further perspectives on unionism.

Still others prefer to express their identity with an L - they are loyalists. Nevertheless they are part of the unionist family.

Moreover, these many parties and organisations - whether political, paramilitary, community or religious - are not themselves monolithic. Within each of these bodies there is a spectrum of beliefs, values and opinions. While the spectrum may be broader in some than in others, it exists in them all. So it seems clear that, while all unionists would share a basic commitment to the maintenance of the Union between Northern Ireland and Great Britain, there is no unionist monolith.

So much is common knowledge; but there is another dimension to unionist identity that is central to the concern of this book.

This identity introduces a new letter to the unionist alphabet - P for Protestant. This letter raises a crucial question: Is Protestantism essential to unionism? Does a political commitment to the cause of the Union go hand in hand with a spiritual - or, at the very least, religious - commitment to Protestantism? After all, many leading unionist politicians are ministers in Protestant churches while many more march as members of organisations that are sworn to maintain and defend Protestantism.

However, in this book we do not propose to analyse or assess - much less answer - these questions. Instead, we offer it as a contribution to a debate, allowing the diverse voices of the unionist people to speak.

The Purpose of this Book

THIS PUBLICATION FORMS PART OF A WIDER ECONI PROJECT ON THE THEME OF *God, Land and Nation* that explores the relationship between religious and political identities. While religious identity has influenced the political identity of both unionism and nationalism, our primary concern is to explore the understanding of the relationship held by people within the unionist tradition in Northern Ireland.

The purpose of this book within that wider project is to give an opportunity to a wide range of individuals from a Protestant or unionist or evangelical Christian background to tell how they see their identity. This is not to say that every contributor is a pro-union Protestant evangelical. Indeed there are a few contributors who feel little or no affinity with any of these identities. However, most would identify themselves as Protestants, most would identify themselves as unionists and a significant number would identify themselves as evangelical Christians.

Specifically, each contributor was asked to respond briefly to the question, What does *For God and Ulster* mean to you? This phrase, with its historical resonance in the unionist community and its linking of Protestant and Ulster identities, provides an ideal focus for reflection on unionist identity and the place of Protestantism within that identity.

The book is also intended to be a contribution toward a better understanding of unionist perspectives on a key aspect of unionist identity. It is also our hope that in time it may serve as an introduction to a wider debate on Protestantism and unionist identity, particularly on the role of evangelical Christianity in establishing or maintaining that identity.

The Contributors

THROUGH THE SUMMER OF 1996 WE CONTACTED 120 PEOPLE, EXPLAINING THE purpose of the book and inviting each to write a brief piece in response to the question, What does For God and Ulster mean to you?

Those invited to contribute fell into the ten broad categories listed below. Needless to say these categories are not rigid, nor are they all equally well represented. However, the categorisation was a useful way of ensuring that invitations were extended to a broad range of individuals.

1. Academic This category includes those who have contributed to academic discussion of matters relating to Northern Ireland. Many of them teach in Northern Ireland's universities across a wide range of disciplines.

2. Arts This category includes novelists, playwrights and poets with roots in the unionist community.

3. Church Leaders This group consists of the leaders of the three main Protestant churches and ministers or leaders from other established Protestant churches as well as some independent churches.

4. Cultural Traditions This category covers those whose work involves research into and promotion of the cultural traditions of the unionist people.

5. Exiles These are people from Northern Ireland who are now living and working outside the country.

6. Loyal Institutions This group consists of members of the Orange Order, the Royal Black Institution, the Apprentice Boys of Derry and the Independent Orange Order.

7. Loyalists In this category are representatives of the Progressive Unionist Party and the Ulster Democratic Party.

8 Outsiders These are people who, though not from Northern Ireland, have a significant interest in the country. As well as being outsiders some are also incomers, having chosen to live and work in Northern Ireland.

9. Politicians This group consists of all pro-Union Members of Parliament and selected members of pro-Union political parties.

10. Youth & Community This category covers those individuals whose work brings them into regular contact with the ordinary men, women and young people who make up so much of the unionist community in all its diversity.

ECONI's goal has been to let others speak and to listen to what they have to say; but we, too, have something to say. Thus one of our contributors is David Hewitt, chairman of ECONI. However, his contribution, like the others, is a personal reflection. It is not a comment on or response to any of the other contributions, none of which he saw before writing his own piece.

While there are a number of members of the ECONI Steering Group among the other contributors they were invited on the basis of other roles they perform or other positions they hold. The biographical note that accompanies each contribution identifies those who are members.

This first process of selection on our part was then followed by a process of self-selection on the part of those invited. To our great encouragement a significant number of those contacted indicated their willingness to contribute. As a consequence the scope and size of the publication increased dramatically. Initially hoping for between twelve and fifteen contributions, we received more than 50. As a result we have been able to present quite a broad cross-section of views and perspectives.

Undoubtedly every reader could suggest others who could make valuable contributions. However, we had to stop somewhere. Moreover, as noted above, our hope is that this book will form the basis for a wider debate on these questions of identity - a debate that will allow many more voices to be heard.

The contributions are arranged in alphabetical order and each follows the same format. While many of the contributors are well known to the general public there are others who may not be quite so familiar, so each piece begins with a brief biographical note. These notes do not provide an account of the origins, associations and achievements of the contributors, but simply help the reader to understand a little better the perspective each contributor brings to the question. Following the biographical note comes the personal reflection. Reading through, you will discover a great diversity of approach and style. Some have taken a personal approach, others write in a more detached manner; some focus on a political analysis, others emphasise the religious dimension.

One final but very important point to note is that each contributor was asked to comment in a personal capacity - What does *For God and Ulster* mean to

you? It must not be assumed that any of these contributions represents the official position of any organisations to which the contributors belong.

Conclusion

I SUSPECT THAT EVERYONE WHO READS THESE PIECES WILL BE OFFENDED BY something. Yet there are many people who hold deeply to each of the views expressed in these pages. Simply ignoring their views will not make them go away. However, I hope that everyone will also be challenged by something. Perhaps if we are challenged to think about the things that offend us we will have a sound basis for continuing the discussion.

I would like to thank all those who contributed to this book. While some are members of the ECONI Steering Group or in broad sympathy with ECONI, there are others who do not see eye to eye with ECONI on many important matters and I particularly appreciate their willingness to contribute to this project.

I would like to encourage those of you who read this book. Specifically, I would like to encourage you to do two things:

1. If you have found it useful, helpful, provocative, or of value in any way, please make others aware of it.

2. If it has stimulated your thinking, expanded your vision or provoked your wrath please let me know. This is a contribution to a debate.

John Alderdice

John Alderdice grew up in Wellington Street Manse in Ballymena. A leader in church youth work, he represented the Presbyterian Church at many national and international committees and conferences. After studies in medicine and psychiatry he was appointed Ireland's first Consultant Psychotherapist. He is also Honorary Lecturer at the Queen's University of Belfast and, since 1993, Medical Director of South and East Belfast Health and Social Services Trust. He has led the Alliance Party since 1987 and is a Belfast City Councillor, a Vice-President of Liberal International and Treasurer of the European Liberals. In October 1996 he was raised to the peerage as Lord Alderdice of Knock. He is an elder in Knock Presbyterian Church in Belfast.

I HAVE ALWAYS HAD AN ENORMOUS PROBLEM with the slogan *For God and Ulster*.

Ulster is home to me, and home is very precious. I travel a good deal these days and I often remark that when I return to London or Dublin I am glad to be somewhere familiar, but until I return to Belfast I am not 'home'. This province is very much my home, and I have given a great deal of myself to working for its welfare.

However, Ulster is not just a place. Unfortunately it is also a term redolent of the themes of traditional unionism and orangeism. These are political positions which I do not share. I find them exclusivist and conservative. The use by republicans like Pearse of the symbols of Christ's Passion to imbue Irish nationalism with religious overtones is similarly unwelcome. De Valera's vision of a Gaelic Catholic Ireland holds no attraction for someone of my convictions. However, it is not my lack of sympathy for the politics of orangeism and nationalism that is at the heart of my unease with the slogan *For God and Ulster*.

The idea that God should be associated with any political entity and its inhabitants - be it Israel, Britain, Ulster or wherever - is completely alien to my reading of the gospel and my understanding of God. The belief that the omniscient, omnipresent God-of-all-being should be identified with one political entity and those who support it would be laughable

FAITH IN ULSTER

if it were not held with such seriousness. To be committed to defending Ulster is a perfectly laudable position, as long as that defence is conducted in a legitimate and Christian way. To be committed to God and His ways is, however, on an entirely different level. I object to the two commitments being spoken of in the same way. That is at the very least primitive, and at the worst sacrilegious.

I do not mean that politics and faith should not mix. My political views are shaped by my faith and convictions. I believe in the dignity of every person. I am certain that we all have both a right and a responsibility to conduct our lives by our principles. I am convinced that we must strive to ensure that our relationships with others are characterised by generosity of spirit. This is not just my political credo; these principles are a part of the expression of my faith in God as He is revealed in Christ. However, there was one element of that revelation which was a problem for the New Testament church.

Christ's proclamation that the gospel was not the property of the Jews, but that He had come for Gentiles, for men and women, clean and unclean, bond and free, was heresy to those who stood *For God and Israel*. But it was the essence of the gospel. Those who stand *For God and Ulster* are trying to tie God to one polity, and to bind the gospel in the chains from which Christ loosed the church when it transcended Judaism. However, the most appalling feature of the *For God and Ulster* mentality is demonstrated when apparently committed Christians line up with individuals and organisations that are corrupt and menacing in the extreme.

God does not need any of us to defend Him, but the behaviour of some of those who claim to be defending Ulster not only fails to promote the cause of Christ, it is actually incompatible with the Christian way. Indeed, it so defiles the cause of Christ that it is an attack on God. Christ, it should be remembered, was not a Zealot. Instead, He calls all of us, as He did Simon, to leave the Zealots and be His disciples in all the world.

Arthur Aughey

Athur Aughey was born in Banbridge. He studied at the Queen's University of Belfast and Hull University. Senior Lecturer in Politics at the University of Ulster at Jordanstown, he is a regular contributor to a wide range of publications in the fields of politics and nationalism. His study of unionist reactions to the Anglo-Irish Agreement, Under Siege: Ulster Unionism and the Anglo-Irish Agreement, was published by Blackstaff in 1989. He is joint editor with Duncan Morrow of Northern Ireland Politics (Longman, 1996). He is a member of the Cadogan Group.

THE MEANING OF THE EXPRESSION *FOR GOD and Ulster* I can understand in a number of distinctive ways. In philosophic mode the phrase poses interesting questions of primacy. Does fidelity to God take precedence over loyalty to place, setting ethical boundaries to the means by which Ulster may be defended? Or is loyalty to Ulster invested with a righteousness which justifies all means to achieve its security? Does the phrase exemplify perfectly Conor Cruise O'Brien's definition of the religious quality of modern nationalism - Godland? All three things are partly true.

In historical mode it is easy to recognise similar sentiments in other examples from the past - 'Faith and Fatherland', *Gott mit uns,* even 'For Harry! England and St George!' And that knowledge of others' historical understanding allows us to ask of ourselves - Whose God? Whose Ulster? On the other hand, in our contemporary political world where spin-doctors believe they can fire the popular imagination with such stunning banalities as 'back to basics' or 'the stakeholder society', it can be seen that *For God and Ulster* expresses a romantic nobility with all the muscular certainty of a world that is gone.

Of course these are very cerebral reflections. For anyone from a Protestant background this phrase is more than an object of contemplation. It may also provoke a sentimental response, even from someone like myself who does not participate in the traditional rites of the Protestant community and who feels as much of an outsider as an insider. How might that response be described? Perhaps the best way to explain it would be to describe my reaction to a loyalist band parade which recently distracted me as I went about a Saturday's shopping.

The sound that summoned me was drums, not bells, and I found it difficult to remain immune to it. Though I would build my shrines to reason and not to God and Ulster I was drawn to the spectacle of Protestant Boys and Young Defenders, to the bravado of these latter-day Sons of Ulster. I followed them - discreetly - as they shouldered their silken martyrs and their icons of civil and religious liberty along the Cregagh Road, down the Woodstock, to turn left onto My Lady's Road. This was Belfast, my Belfast, transformed into Belfast, their Belfast. Here was naked noisesome assertion - incorrigible and unapologetic. As the music faded I can admit to feeling briefly a strange kind of loss. For however much my liberal conscience might rebel, what I had experienced was not an alien practice. It was also another part of me. To paraphrase Terence I might say: I am of the Ulster Protestant community and count nothing of that community indifferent to me.

In my general state of ironic intellectual detachment I have little time for either God or Ulster. Yet a greater irony is this: the sound of a loyalist band can stir emotions and identifications which are not simply momentary, not simply illusory, but real. "The accent of one's birthplace," as La Rochefoucauld said, "persists in the mind and heart as much as in speech."

Glen Barr

Between 1973-76 and 1978-81 Glen
Barr was Senior Political Spokesman for
the Ulster Defence Association. In 1974
he chaired the Ulster Loyalist Central
Co-ordinating Committee which
organised and controlled the 1974
Constitutional Stoppage, commonly
known as the Workers' Strike. In
Beyond the Religious Divide (1979)
he argued the case for a sovereign
independent Northern Ireland. Currently
a member of the Community Relations
Council and Londonderry City
Partnership, he has founded or co-
founded a wide range of groups
involved in community and business
development and community relations
including the Waterside Area
Partnership, the Ulster Community
Action Network and the Maydown
Ebrington Group.

A CHILD'S REPLY from THE LAMENTATIONS OF
MOTHER ULSTER

Oh my mother, how my heart weeps for you
And all that you have suffered.
Your beauty has been scarred
By the centuries of blood and tramping invading
feet.
You have been used and abused by successive suitors
For their own selfish ends.
You have been betrayed by so-called friends
And deserted by those who knew your love.

Yet it is not these things which fill my heart with
pain,
For they needed not the words of a prophet to
predict.
It is how the memories have left you lonely and
bitter.
I knew the scars were deep,
So much so you hid your beauty for shame.
But the words of despair that now reach my ears
Are not from the womb from whence I came.

Oh my mother, you know I will not desert you,
Or allow you to be taken against your will.
But the times have changed,
And our problems can no longer be solved by the
sword.
Cuchulain must continue his sleep,
And we, your children that are left,
Must find the answer.

In our search for the answer we must first find the Light,
For only the Light can show us the path.
When we emerge from our darkness to walk in the ways of God,
Then we will find peace and prosperity.
For in our darkness
We face each other with hatred and suspicion,
Not believing that we are one.
We seek victory for earthly symbols
Believing they represent God.
But God is not interested in the symbols of man
And cries for your children
To seek out the Truth.

Woe to those clerics and others who have used His name
In ways that are not His to divide your children.
They have made them believe
That their side is right and the other side wrong,
That their word is true and the other word false,
That they shall be accepted and the other rejected,
That they can kill in His name because they are His chosen.

Hypocrites! Antichrists!
How can they claim to know God's children
When they themselves don't know God?
Only they who have known the Risen Life, the Lamb of Peace,
And follow the example of God's beloved Son
Shall be called the Children of God.
Oh my mother,
If you are to be saved from the chains of bondage,
If you are to be lifted from the depths of despair,
Your children must be prepared to travel
Through their present state of darkness

Into the light of God's world.
And when the Lord of Hosts is exalted
To His rightful place throughout our land,
Only then will you know His love and mercy,
Only then will you know His saving grace.

We all love you my Mother,
In our divided earthly ways.
And the day will come
When the Harp and Crown will leave us in peace,
And through the Risen Life, and
Our common love for you,
We will rebuild our home together.

There is none on earth to compare with you,
You are Ulster.
You are my mother.

Geoffrey Beattie

Geoffrey Beattie was born in Ligoniel and educated at the Belfast Royal Academy and the University of Birmingham. He obtained a doctorate in Psychology from the University of Cambridge. He is now Professor of Psychology at the University of Manchester. He has written nine books, including works on psychology, and descriptions of mainly working-class life in Britain today. He has also written about his background in Belfast in We are the People: Journeys Through the Heart of Protestant Ulster *(Heinemann, 1992). He is currently engaged in psychological research on a number of aspects of human communication and is working on a novel.*

THERE WAS A FRONT ROOM AND A BACK ROOM. This was the backroom. It overlooked the yard. I was seven years old before I managed to climb over the yard wall for the first time. My older brother taught me how to do it. You had to open the toilet door until it was level with Donaghy's wall. Then you put your left foot on the top of the middle panel in the door, then your right foot in this little cleft in the middle of Donaghy's wall, then you swung your left leg onto the corrugated iron roof. It was slippy, especially in winter, so you had to scramble along the roof, using both your hands and your feet. But it was worth it. You could see right into Ella Gordon's yard and the Donaghy's yard from up there. Yards were private. There was no back door onto the entry. You carried your bin out through the front room. It was a sign of maturity when you could carry the full bin outstretched in front of you, out through the front door without hitting the furniture. I liked sitting on the yard wall. It was the only glimpse of those other yards that you ever had.

The yards of Limepark Street backed onto ours. My mother always told us that young girls lived in the house directly opposite ours. She used to tell us that they had 'a quare view'. In winter instead of running to the toilet my brother and I would sometimes send out a great gleaming golden arc onto the frosty paving stones. According to my mother these young girls of indeterminate number and age would watch diligently as we did this.

The backroom had a dresser, a chest of drawers and a bed with three legs. The other leg had buckled at some time in the past. It was still there, according to my mother, it just needed fixed. My brother said that if it was somewhere in that dark hole below the bed, then it was beyond repair. It was alright for him, I had to sleep in that dip. You had to try and level yourself with your shoulder until sleep came. The bed was always damp.

We had a paraffin stove. We called it 'the heater'. We used to buy the paraffin out the back of the Post Office. The stove gave off fumes, but I loved that smell. It was always warm and inviting. But the fumes quickly gave you a headache. *For God and Ulster* was written on the gable wall. Sometimes. Along with other slogans that reminded you where you were, and who you were. Our side - King Billy, Ulster, and apparently God; their side the Pope, Ireland and God knows what. I knew little about the Church of Rome. *For God and Ulster* was just a slogan hinting that we could work or fight for God and Ulster simultaneously, that there was no essential contradiction between these two things, that we were in some sense on the right side. "We are the people," we said unselfconsciously. The people with everything. I used to lie in my bed in Legmore street and ponder this. It seemed strange.

But *For God and Ulster* has always been more than a slogan or sound-bite, more than just a summary of a position. If you want to understand what a word or phrase means you need to look at how it is used. It's the *for* that gives the game away in this particular case. *For God and Ulster* is giving the reason for something. It may be evoked to tell you why something was done. It is an attribution, already handily packaged, easy to access, easy to use. It is a convenient and ready-made justification. It can be an excuse. For whatever actions.

Even then.

Eileen Bell

Eileen Bell was born in County Down and raised in West Belfast. A graduate of the New University of Ulster in History and Politics, she is currently Vice-Chairman of the Alliance Party of Northern Ireland and the Party's spokesman on education. She is a member of the Northern Ireland Forum and the Alliance Party's negotiating team at the multi-party talks. In the 1992 Westminster election she contested the Newry & Armagh constituency. In 1993 she was elected to North Down Borough Council. At the height of the IRA campaign against the Belfast - Dublin rail link she joined with a number of others to form the Peace Train Organisation.

I MUST ADMIT THAT MY FIRST REACTION TO THE phrase *For God and Ulster* is to dismiss it out of hand as one of a group that includes 'A Protestant Parliament for a Protestant People' and 'Ulster Will Fight and Ulster Will be Right'. These phrases denote a brand of intolerance that is intolerable.

This initial reaction can be put down to the fact that, although I would term myself a person of unionist inclination, I abhor all expressions that might show triumphalism or discrimination as this phrase appears to me to do. I realise that this in itself is a very generalised viewpoint and that many people do hold a genuine perception that this expression represents all that is traditional and good in their cultural and ethical background. Nevertheless it has been used once too often by those who want to intimidate for it to be free of any taint of intolerance. My personal experience is of hearing it being used as an excuse for forcing myself and my husband out of our home in the early seventies because of our 'mixed marriage'.

I am not a natural unionist in that I was born into a Catholic family from the Falls Road and should really have developed into a republican or nationalist, aspiring to a united Ireland. This did not happen, because I was lucky to have been born into a family that put human dignity and civil rights for all before the restricting perspectives of political cant or ideology. We were Catholics, but we never saw other religious beliefs as threats or evils and I therefore had the added advantage that I saw other people as individuals first and Catholics, Protestants, unionists or nationalists later - and then only when it was necessary.

I therefore did not need the comfort or support of slogans such as *For God and Ulster* or *Eirean go Bragh* because I was able to develop my own thought processes and learn by my experience as a committed Christian. I am also confident of my identity as a native of Northern Ireland, seeing the richness of its diversity as a sign of strength. I do not see the need to threaten any of my fellow citizens with any sort of force, verbal or otherwise.

I have to admit, though, to trying to live up to one slogan, "Love God and your neighbour - do unto others as you would have them do unto you." I think that covers a multitude of vices and virtues that can help me deal with life in Northern Ireland today.

Esmond Birnie

Esmond Birnie is a university lecturer in Economics and holds degrees from Cambridge University and the Queen's University of Belfast. He is co-author of a number of publications on competitiveness and productivity in Eastern Europe and Ireland, as well as publications considering the relationship between Christianity and capitalism. He is the co-author with Patrick J Roche of An Economics Lesson for Irish Nationalists and Republicans (Ulster Unionist Information Institute, 1995) arguing the economic case for the Union. He was Deputy-Chairman of the Conservative Party in Northern Ireland (1995-96) but resigned because of his conviction that the Party had failed to adopt a consistent and honourable pro-Union policy. He is now a member of the Ulster Unionist Party.

"HIS FAITH WOULD LIE IN GOD AND FREEDOM, and in the influence of Great Britain as asserting both." Thus said the Liberal Prime Minister, Lord Rosebery, of Oliver Cromwell at the dedication in 1899 of a statue of the latter in Parliament Square. As the Bible makes abundantly clear, political states have roles in God's plans and, just like individuals, can be subjected to His judgment.

Of course God does not need the United Kingdom, Republic of Ireland, America, Germany or any other state to accomplish His purposes, but it seems He has decided to use them. Moreover, a plausible reading of the biblical and extra-biblical evidence seems to suggest that a plurality of political states has been part of God's strategy to arrest humanity's capacity to do evil.

Indeed, it could be argued that patriotism, along with the family, legal systems and the market economy are devices which God has given us in order to channel often destructive and selfish human nature towards more constructive ends. Love for one's country can be perverted, as can love for one's family, but without it life in this world would approach more closely to the small scale hell Augustine feared it was.

There is, admittedly, nothing inherent in reformed or evangelical Chrsitianty which necessarily commits its adherents to unionism. There are, however, compelling reasons why we should still favour this option:

1. Most people in Northern Ireland enjoy a much better standard of living as part of the UK than they would under any conceivable all-Ireland arrangements.

2. Conversely, any moves within the next 10-15 years towards a united Ireland would place intolerable burdens on the already long suffering taxpayers of the Republic.

3. The UK has a reasonable track record in accommodating ethnic diversity. The capacity of the Republic in this respect is at best untried.

4. While a number of characteristics of the 1921 - 1972 Stormont regime were indeed shameful, three things should be remembered: first, Carson and Craig preferred integration with the rest of the UK in 1921 but devolution was imposed on them by Lloyd George; second, the position of the Catholic minority in Northern Ireland probably compared very favourably with the lot of various national minorities in eastern Europe; third, since 1968 huge efforts have been made to address perceived unfairness with respect to social, educational and job matters. Notwithstanding this, the IRA campaign continued.

5. If militant Republicanism achieves one victory by breaking the link with Britain its next objective would be the the revolutionary replacement of the government in Dublin.

6. Since 1985 Northern Ireland has been moved by stealth towards a situation of joint rule by both London and Dublin. This situation of government without consent is fundamentally unfair. It is a strange sort of 'parity of esteem' which allows the Dublin Government to be an active exponent for unity whereas its UK counterpart declares it has no interest in the continuation of the Union.

7. The solution to other national minority problems within the European Union has involved the acceptance of frontiers rather than dishonest attempts to conjure them away.

None of the above is to deny that the Republic and the whole of the UK do have some common interests. Perhaps these could receive institutional expression through some sort of a Council for the Islands of Britain and Ireland.

Finally, it is important to distinguish the political - and ideological - leadership of a country from its people. I drafted this piece in the beautiful imperial German city of Regensburg. It is possible to appreciate greatly many aspects of post-1700 German culture and yet be heartily glad that the several attempts by Germany to dominate our continent failed. In the same way, it should be possible to be a British patriot and also to love Ireland.

David Bleakley

David Bleakley worked as an engineer in Harland & Wolff before going on to study at Oxford University and the Queen's University of Belfast. He was a Northern Ireland Labour Party Member of Parliament at Stormont and served as Minister of Community Relations. An Anglican, he is currently President of the Church Mission Society and has been actively involved in the Irish Council of Churches. He is a former Senior Lecturer in Peace Studies at Bradford University and is currently a member of the Fellowship of Reconciliation, Convenor of the Peace Pledge Ireland Group and President of the Christian Socialist Fellowship. He has written a number of books, most recently Peace in Ireland: Two States One People *(Mowbray-Cassell, 1995).*

TOWARDS A POLITICS OF PARTNERSHIP

As a Christian Socialist seeking to build a united Northern Ireland based on caring and sharing I do not favour slogans like *For God and Ulster* - nor, indeed, any 'wearing of the green' version. Both are divisive.

Religion means a striving for personal salvation combined with service to our neighbours. Such obligations lie at the heart of the gospel and proclaim our Lord's sovereignty over the whole creation. In such service we stand alongside those who are at the sharp end of suffering. This 'bias to the poor' puts us in the presence of the Kingdom of God.

My pilgrimage into the affairs of Church and State began in Belfast as a child in pre-war depression years. My earliest memories are of hard times. Even then I felt the unfair contradictions of society: so much poverty alongside the consumption of conspicuous wealth. In our radical Christian family my father proclaimed it a duty to strive against social injustice: "It is your duty to seek the remedy for social injustice; and with God's help you will find it." Keir Hardie's vision was often quoted: "Christian Socialism is the reign of love in the room of hate. It is woven from the same loom as was the vision of Isaiah and is also, without doubt, of the same texture as that Kingdom of God which the early Christians believed to be at hand." This vision is still an inspiration to those seeking a society based on the twin pillars of caring and sharing. Nowadays it is a vision of witness which takes centre stage in the Councils of the worldwide Church.

However, beyond the call to wider witness we are also required to be aware of local community obligations. For this reason Christian Socialists in Northern Ireland have always sought to build across the sectarian divide. In my formative years I was taught to question preachers who turned religion into an 'opiate of the people'. In those days we were pioneers and the reconciliation sought between Protestants and Roman Catholics was not called 'ecumenism'. To us it was just decent commonsense and a mark of shared humanity.

Peacemaking pioneers were, then as now, often viewed with suspicion by what my radical father called 'the Orange / Green establishment'. He regarded their sectarianism as incompatible with Christian behaviour. As Sadie Patterson put it in a pungent comment: "Religion is an accident of birth. Bigotry - leave it aside. It went out with hobble skirts and button boots." The advice was homespun, but it had a lasting effect on my generation. Had it been heeded more widely there would have been no 1969. Nor would we be living in fear of another Drumcree or the tribal boycotts and burnings-out which beset us.

We still have time, but it is no longer on our side. Like the priest in *Cry the Beloved Country,* "I have one great fear in my heart, that one day when they turn to loving they will find that we have turned to hating."

These are grave and sombre words drawing attention to the unfinished business facing politicians in contemporary Ireland.

Yet Christian hope is total hope, touching all aspects of life, both individual and social. Even at the darkest moments of our 'Troubles' we have had glimpses of a better way of doing things: human acts of forgiveness, even from those who have suffered most; the shared joy and relief which accompanied the ceasefires; the vision and courage of Brian Faulkner who became our most ecumenical leader in power-sharing. Together we have seen a new future and know that it can work. For those who strive for a Northern Ireland at peace with itself and at ease with its neighbours the proclamation of that hope is not an empty dream.

Ken Bloomfield

Sir Ken Bloomfield was born in Belfast in 1931 and educated at the Royal Belfast Academical Institution and Oxford University. During a long career in the Civil Service he headed the Northern Ireland Government's office in the United States, served with a number of Cabinet Ministers in Stormont and worked closely with three successive Prime Ministers - O'Neill, Chichester-Clark and Faulkner. In 1974 he served as Secretary to the power-sharing Executive. After serving as Permanent Secretary in a number of Government Departments, he became head of the Northern Ireland Civil Service in 1984. He retired in 1991. He is the author of Stormont in Crisis: A Memoir *(Blackstaff, 1994).*

IT IS A CHALLENGE TO HAVE BEEN ASKED HOW IN today's circumstances I react to the slogan *For God and Ulster.* I have to be frank and say that I am unsympathetic to any inference that the interests of God and Ulster are in some way necessarily synonymous. The history of the world is steeped in the blood of people who sincerely believed that their interests were uniquely well-aligned with those of the Supreme Being. In this belief Christian killed Jew, Muslim killed Christian, Hindu killed Muslim and adherents of particular Christian churches killed each other - all, in some dreadful sense, 'in good faith'. I have grown to dislike and even to fear slogans and easy cant phrases.

We speak often, do we not, of 'our glorious heritage'? Yet very often it amounts to little more than the repetitive commemoration of divisiveness and suspicion. I feel, from time to time, that I would dearly like to take our accumulated baggage of phoney religio-patriotic nostalgia and sink it in the deepest ocean.

I just do not find it intellectually credible or emotionally tolerable to believe that God could or would have singled out any minority of human kind for a singular favour and a special destiny. Rather do I believe that all human beings everywhere are called to place upon their animal natures - greedy and ferocious as they often are - the restraint of that self-respect which best shows itself in respect for other people. Ulster at times is rancid with the insensitive demands which arise out of pure self-interest. When lay people descend into communal selfishness, it is a cause for disappointment; when political or religious leaders do so, it is a betrayal of some basic tenets of the religion most of us share.

It is a mistake to suppose that the tragic divisions apparent in our society can be overcome through some grand, high-level political solution. Tolerance cannot be decreed by fiat, or mutual respect imposed by codes of law. Ulster can only be moved out of the Serbonian bog of discord by a rebirth, in the hearts and minds of countless people, of values which are more often paraded than observed. The Beatitudes are likely to be a more reliable pointer to a positive future than Ulster's Solemn League and Covenant or the Anglo-Irish Agreement. If, in the best sense, we are for God, I suspect that Ulster will take care of itself.

Myrtle Boal

Myrtle Boal was born in Northern Ireland and educated at Ashleigh House School in Belfast. She was sales manager for Ireland with a multi-national pharmaceutical company until 1994. A member of the Conservative Party, she contested the East Antrim seat in the 1993 Westminster election and was the Conservative candidate in the 1994 European election. She is currently Chairman of the South Belfast Conservative Association and works for a smaller pharmaceutical company with responsibility for Northern Ireland. She is a member of the Crescent Church and a member and Past-President of Soroptomist International of Belfast.

EACH OF US IS BORN INTO A FAMILY FROM WHICH we take our name, and into a nation, from which we take our passport. Family and national identities are established. It is right and proper that kinship, love, support, protection and a sense of belonging should be experienced inside those systems. It is equally right that love, kinship, loyalty and commitment to those systems should be reciprocated.

Many of us born in the Northern part of Ireland, while having a political identity as part of the United Kingdom, identify also with the rest of the island. Geographically, the British Isles is a single entity. Culturally, it splits into Scots, Welsh, English and Irish. Politically, it splits into the United Kingdom and the Republic of Ireland. It follows that one can be British-Irish as much as British-Scottish or British-English. I am proud to be Irish and proud to be British.

When one becomes a Christian one acquires citizenship in God's Kingdom and an extra dimension comes into being. Added to family and national identity is spiritual identity, bringing greater love, requiring greater loyalty and embracing not only this life but the life beyond. Are these loyalties mutually exclusive? Can one love, and be loyal to, one's family, one's country and one's God? What is required of us? What does the Bible say?

For God and My Country

In the Bible we are exhorted to be good citizens, giving respect, tax and loyalty where due. Jesus exhorted us to "render to Caesar the things that are Caesar's and to God the things that are God's" - this to a people living under a ruthless foreign power that had conquered their country.

Today we have the privilege of democracy - a privilege worth defending. While no country is fairer to its citizens than the United Kingdom, sadly, in this part of the Kingdom, some who have benefited from the largesse of our country have tried to overthrow by force the democratically elected government. Because of the United Kingdom's sense of fair play, our government has bent over backwards to listen to and accommodate this lawless, ungrateful minority, compromising the loyal, law abiding majority, who continue to suffer silently. In successive elections we have voted overwhelmingly to maintain the constitutional status quo; our love and loyalty has been and still is to the United Kingdom.

As our country has been bombed, our policemen killed, our economy all but ruined, only our commitment to "that other country whose paths are peace" has prevented individuals, frustrated by our government's ambivalence, from taking the law into their own hands and turning Ulster into another Bosnia. Our commitment to God has been greater than, and has superseded, our own commitment to Ulster. We have turned the other cheek more than once. We have forgiven seventy times seven. Now, having bombed their way close to the negotiating table, these people of violence have embarked on a new strategy to rob us of our citizenship. Only God knows the outcome of this conflict.

However, we know that our membership of God's family, our citizenship of that other country, is safe from attack. Nothing can separate us from the love of Christ - not now, not never.

Yes, for God and for my country.

Gareth Burke

Gareth Burke was born in Belfast and educated at the Queen's University of Belfast and the Free Church of Scotland College, Edinburgh. He has been a minister in the Evangelical Presbyterian Church since 1984, first at Somerton Road, Belfast and, since 1989, at Knock, Belfast.

As a child the slogan *For God and Ulster* meant nothing to me. It was never used in our home and my only acquaintance with it was when I saw it painted on gable walls. With the passing of the years I came to realise that this phrase is precious to many Ulster Protestants, one which they feel succinctly summarises their position both politically and religiously.

They are for God - for the God of the Bible, for the God of the Reformers, for the God of William III. To be for God, they maintain, means that one must also be for Ulster - for the Ulster that is part of the United Kingdom with its Protestant throne, for the Ulster that maintains a separate existence from the Irish Republic dominated, they maintain, by the Church of Rome. *For God and Ulster* is the watchword of Ulster Protestants who maintain that the Protestant reformed religion and the cause of Ulster unionism are one and the same thing.

My own response to this phrase is twofold.

Firstly, I feel a certain amount of confusion. The British throne to which Ulster Protestants claim allegiance is rapidly becoming non-Protestant. The heir to the throne is an enthusiast for multi-faith services and the New Age movement. He is most unlikely to be willing to take a solemn oath to maintain and defend the Protestant religion. Should we claim allegiance to a throne that is rapidly departing from the Protestant faith? Should we long to remain part of a nation that is godless and secular? Many of those who are foremost in the cause of Ulster unionism have no living faith in Jesus Christ and no true appreciation of the teaching of the Word of God. How can we view them as defenders of the faith?

Secondly, I am fully committed to the Protestant reformed religion. I believe that the Bible is the Word of God. I believe that Jesus Christ is the only saviour of sinners. I am opposed to the doctrine and worship of the Church of Rome and abhor all forms of false ecumenism. I recognise that the true people of God, those who have faith in Jesus Christ, are found in many different churches. Yet I belong to a separatist church because I believe that such a position is taught in the Word of God. I long for God to pour out His blessing on our land and nation and am aware that He is, as the sovereign God, actively involved in the affairs of the nations.

Yet I could not use this slogan personally for I do not feel that the cause of God and the cause of Ulster are necessarily synonymous. Unionism is a legitimate cause and an acceptable political position to which I adhere, but to be a Christian in Ulster today does not automatically mean that one must be a unionist. We can never say to someone, "You must believe in the Lord Jesus Christ and, as a Christian, be committed to the cause of Ulster." This is to impose a burden on new believers for which there is no biblical warrant. It is almost as serious as the error of adding to the gospel which Paul so strongly refutes in his letter to the Galatians. People need to seek Christ and to believe in Him by faith. It may be that they will hold a unionist position politically, but we can never impose this upon them.

We want men and women to be for God but we can never insist that they must automatically be for Ulster.

Gregory Campbell

Gregory Campbell was elected to the City Council in Londonderry in 1981. He is a member of the Democratic Unionist Party and the Party's security spokesman. He was part of the DUP talks team during the 1991-2 constitutional discussions and is also involved in the current multi-party talks. He has contested the Foyle Constituency in the last three Parliamentary elections. He is the author of a number of booklets on discrimination against the Protestant community and the political situation in Northern Ireland.

THE TERM *FOR GOD AND ULSTER* FIRST CAME into common usage in the early part of this century when the men of Carson's Ulster Volunteer Force adopted it as their unofficial watchword to sum up their Protestant religious fervour and their patriotism.

For me the slogan is properly used in the context of a beleaguered, embattled people having been so vilified and so misrepresented that they must seek a refuge which will not betray them. The evangelical witness in Northern Ireland has had a long and illustrious past with such figures as Henry Cook, 'Roaring' Hugh Hanna and WP Nicholson. These men were prominent Protestant churchmen who epitomised the slogan before its coinage became current.

Unfortunately the term has been considerably devalued in recent years because of its use in association with some whose activities include the drugs trade, racketeering and so-called punishment beatings. However, there is still merit in its use today despite this; despite, too, the recent trend to dismiss it as a slogan more in keeping with an almost pre-historic era when the members of each tribe called upon their god to support them in a fight to the death with the other.

For God and Ulster is a term which sits uneasily in a modern world with no sense of direction or purpose and which prefers to accommodate everyone with everything rather than proclaim a particular truth and stand by it no matter what. The term is a powerful affirmation of belief in a sovereign God who disposes that which puny people propose. Those who shun it completely in the belief that it sectarianises the gospel either do not understand or do not accept the essential nature of the dispute between Protestantism and Roman Catholicism.

The major drawback for those of us who are proud of the slogan is that both it and the surrounding loyalist historical baggage that goes with it are accused of being irrelevant to modern society, or of not being beneficial to generations of Protestants now leaving school or starting families - sometimes both at the same time.

Yet one of the most important tasks facing Christians in today's society, as it stands on the verge of social and spiritual meltdown, is to get across the wonderful news that Jesus Christ died as a sacrifice for our sins, in a way that is relevant to this generation.

Can that be done in a way which neither detracts from Ulster's British identity nor minimises one's allegiance to it? I am one of those who passionately believes that it can.

Fred Catherwood

Sir Fred Catherwood was born in Castledawson. Following study at Cambridge he qualified as a chartered accountant. He has been successively chief executive of Costain, British Aluminium and John Laing. He was Director General of the National Economic Development Council (1966-71), Chairman of the Institute of Management (1974-76) and Chairman of the British Overseas Trade Board (1975-79). From 1979 to 1994 he was a Member of the European Parliament and its Vice-President from 1989-1992. He is currently President of the Evangelical Alliance and Vice-President of the International Fellowship of Evangelical Students. Among his books are The Christian in Industrial Society *(Tyndale Press, 1964) and his memoirs,* At the Cutting Edge *(Hodder & Stoughton, 1995).*

WHEN PAGANISM LAST SPREAD ACROSS ENGLAND 1,500 years ago, Ireland remained Christian. Columba crossed the water from Ireland to convert the Scots and Scottish missionaries went south to convert the pagan English. Today, once more, paganism is spreading across England and, once more, the Christian faith is strongest in the island of Ireland - especially in the North - where more people go to church, there is less crime and, despite the paramilitaries, the streets are far safer than they are on the mainland. And yet in the world at large the Christian faith in Ireland is, tragically, a byword for bigotry.

We feel that, while Irish Christianity is not faultless, this judgment is unfair. I asked an old colleague who had just come back to Whitehall after a spell in Stormont whether he realised that the trouble was political rather than religious. He told me he did. He related how early on, while dining with a minister in the Culloden Hotel, the manager reported that the Protestant women of west Belfast were outside. They had their wee boys with them and their wee boys had half-bricks and they wanted to see the minister. When the women came in my friend said to them, "I'm not much of a Christian, but I know that Christians are meant to love their neighbours and you want to shoot them." They replied, "We're not Christians, we're Protestants."

Of course there is a good political case

for unionism, as there is for nationalism. The problem arises from one of the last quick-fixes for which Lloyd-George had a genius (the infamous Versailles Treaty being another). With a bit more time an ethnic boundary might have been fixed which allowed the great majority of both unionists and nationalists to be where they wanted without incommoding the other. But the quick fix had to be partition on county boundaries which left an uncomfortably large nationalist minority on the wrong side of the border. It was a time bomb which went off when, after two generations, the minority could no longer tolerate a one party monopoly of government.

At a time when these pressures were building up I spoke in the Whitla Hall at the Queen's University of Belfast. It was packed with students. I urged them not to take to the streets because they would find those beside them who understood the streets better than they did and who would use them to take over. It says a lot for the continued efforts of the churches that though violence did take over it has been held in check.

For we Christians do understand that the second great command is that we should love our neighbours as ourselves - illustrated by Jesus in the parable of the good Samaritan. The Jews and Samaritans each believed the other to be heretical. Alongside this there was a dispute about territory. The Jews and Samaritans were rather like the Catholic Irish and Protestant Ulster-Scots.

But they were neighbours. They had to show the love that the good Samaritan showed to the wounded Jew. We, too, are neighbours.

George Crory

George Crory comes originally from Banbridge where he was educated at the local Academy. After training at Stranmillis College he took up at teaching appointment in Newry. Some years later he entered the Irish Baptist College to train for the Christian ministry. Following nine years as pastor of Finaghy Baptist Church he went to France where another nine years were spent in church planting work. He has now returned home and is currently pastor of the Antrim Road Baptist Church in North Belfast.

LOOKING BACK THROUGH THE YEARS WE CAN all recall certain experiences that made such a strong impression on us we have never forgotten them. For me one such experience was the first time I saw the words *For God and Ulster*. It happened some thirty years ago in the town of Newry where I lived and worked as a young schoolteacher. The words were printed in bold red letters on an election poster, the inference being that if I voted for the party concerned I would be pleasing God, because God was apparently deeply concerned that Ulster should remain British!

I had no theological training at the time (and was none the worse for that) but I do remember being forced to think through and discuss with others certain salient points. As best as I can recall they included the following:

1. Many of the leaders of the political party concerned were well known evangelicals. Was such a slogan, then, true to evangelical and biblical faith?

2. I had many friends who would most certainly not be voting for the party concerned. Did this mean that by so doing they would be sinning against God?

3. I had been familiar with the relationship as depicted in the Old Testament between God and the nation of Israel - "...prepare to meet thy God, O Israel" (Amos 4.12). Were these

posters trying to say that the six counties of Ulster had in some way become a 'New Israel'?

Over the years I have become increasingly concerned with this 'political god' in our society. I could give many reasons why but let me conclude with just three.

1. Jim Packer in his book *Knowing God* says this: "...churchmen who look at God, so to speak, through the wrong end of the telescope, so reducing him to pygmy proportions, cannot hope to end up as more than pygmy Christians." Using the holy name of a sovereign God as a political slogan which projects Him as some sort of 'God of Ulster' is, in my opinion, doing just that.

2. The concept of a theocracy with God ruling over a specific nation state - as in the Old Testament - is no longer relevant today. The Kingdom which Jesus came to announce (Mark 1.14) was not a kingdom in any geographical sense but rather the rule of God in the hearts of men and women. The key to this Kingdom is turned, not by nationality, but by repentance and faith in the Son of God (John 3.3).

3. If we are truly to follow the will of God in this land we must commence the mammoth task of taking politics out of our religious beliefs in order to reach those of every persuasion and none. It is my opinion that the type of thinking behind the phrase *For God and Ulster* has hindered us from doing so for far too long.

Tony Crowe

Tony Crowe is a teacher and community activist in Londonderry. He is Chairman of the Diamond Trust, a body set up to assist in the regeneration of the small Protestant community on the west bank of the Foyle and to help preserve the unique culture of that community. He is also Chairman of the District Partnership and a member of the City Council's Cultural Sub-Committee. A member of the General Committee of the Apprentice Boys of Derry, he chaired the Tercentenary Committee. A historian, he has written A Maiden Still, *a number of booklets to mark the Tercentenary and articles published in numerous political and cultural journals.*

AFTER THE LONG AND DISCONTENTED SUMMER of '96 it is appropriate to reflect on many things, not least the rallying cry *For God and Ulster.*

Coupling homage to the maker with patriotism is not peculiar to Ulster. It is, however, difficult to explain its significance for the individual. Many fellow-Ulstermen interpret our conflict as a religious struggle between good and evil. I regard this as flawed because it detracts from the wider reality of the conflict and the problem of confused identities. This confusion is highlighted when anything to do with 'Ulster' is considered - one only has to reflect that Ulster as an entity, geographically and politically, is divided between two jurisdictions, each of which has traditionally maintained a very different ethos.

My sense of Ulsterness was heightened earlier than most because I was born and spent formative years in that part of Ulster where the reigning jurisdiction supported an alien culture to that of my kinsfolk. Their origins were in the seventeenth century plantation of Donegal. The fact that we were "as native as any here" (John Hewitt) does not detract from another fact - that I was conscious of things that rendered us different from our neighbours. I now recognise that these traditions and values contributed to what I cherish as an integral part of my Ulster identity. I am also convinced that, in a convoluted way, this identity is allied closely to my religious observation.

Vacations with relatives in the South and terms of study in Dublin during the sixties reinforced my awareness of Ulster as a special, separate place. My Southern peers accepted the good currency of this separation for they expressed total disinterest in Ireland's Northern regions. At that time I encountered the work of historian James Good who, in 1919, observed that "leaving politics aside, the special conditions of Ulster life operate in exactly the same fashion on Nationalists as on Unionists, differentiating them from their fellow countrymen in the South...[I]n speech, in temper, in outlook, the Ulsterman of all creeds contrasts more sharply with the natives of the other provinces than the Black Country does with the Home Counties...."

Despite all that has happened, I remain convinced that Good's interpretation is as valid today as it was then. The war of attrition involving so much ethnic cleansing has served to emphasise this reality. While I do not believe that there is a pure national identity, I am certain that increased awareness of Ulster history and culture has helped us through some of our darkest days.

A profound influence on my understanding of my identity has been the work of Dr Ian Adamson. His research has clarified much of the mythology and ambiguity concerning Ulster's past and its current role. I have tried to cultivate a greater appreciation of his work and have been actively involved in the formation of groups like the Ulster Society, dedicated to pursuing at least some of his themes.

On a personal note I am convinced that my pride in Ulster's history and culture has strengthened my belief that Ulster is worth living and - in extreme circumstances - worth dying for. Moreover, I believe that such patriotism could not survive without the strength of God's love. My struggle to find such precious exaltation has evolved almost naturally in parallel with the maturing of my identity as an Ulsterman. My religious beliefs, like my sense of 'Ulsterness' are often very confused, but to quote the schoolmaster in Brian Friel's *Translations* - "confusion is not an ignoble condition."

The exhortation *For God and Ulster* is frequently denigrated by cynics; I conclude by recommending that Ulster cannot survive without God. I know that I would be unfaithful to my sincere aspirations as an Ulsterman if I ignored this fact.

John Dickinson

John Dickinson is a minister of the

Presbyterian Church in Ireland. He

was born in Belfast in 1954 and

grew up in Londonderry. Educated

at Foyle College and the Queen's

University of Belfast he obtained

honours degrees in Arts and

Theology. Ordained by the

Presbytery of East Belfast in 1980,

he served as Assistant Minister in

Bloomfield, Belfast and Minister in

First Killyleagh (1982-1987) and

Seaview, Belfast (1987-). He was

appointed Clerk of the Presbytery of

North Belfast in 1991. He has also

taught Church History part-time at

Belfast Bible College.

"LOOK AT THIS!" MY FRIEND WAS WHISPERING. We were in O-level English class and we were bored. His right hand was under the desk and my attention was drawn to the small oval-shaped metal badge, coppery brown in colour, which was in his palm. "It's an original," he went on, his voice warm with pride. I'd never seen a Ulster Volunteer Force badge before. I took it, lifted it closer to get a better look, and fingered the inscription round the perimeter - *For God and Ulster.*

For my irreligious friend that badge was just something cool - a major advantage in the ongoing game of school one-upmanship. For me, a young Christian, a convinced Protestant, a fervent loyalist, that motto resonated. It was like an incantation which summoned from the pit of history the faith of my forefathers - their principled resistance to submersion in an alien way of life; their readiness to voluntarily sacrifice everything for the safety of the Empire - a readiness immortalised in the mud of no-man's land at the Somme; their unflagging conviction that their cause had Divine Right.

These were heady images for someone growing up in the Maiden City at a time when, it seemed, a majority of its residents were in open rebellion against the lawful authorities. And in course of time it was the same essential convictions which led to involvement in unionist politics and the loyal orders.

Even after a quarter of a century that slogan, along with the sight of an Orange banner or the sound of a flute band, still calls to something primeval in me. Ulster is my home, loyalism my culture. But other convictions have also been born in the interim. Maybe it was listening to Bob Dylan:

For you don't count the dead
when God's on your side,

and Paul Brady:

Up here we sacrifice our children
to feed the worn out dreams of yesterday,

that helped me to think about the price we have paid for our community loyalty to competing theocracies on this island. Maybe it was the growing realisation that the motto divorces the Old and New Testaments, for it sits more easily with the God of Abraham, Isaac and Jacob than with the God and Father of our Lord Jesus Christ. Maybe it was the discovery that investing political arrangements with divine imperatives makes all reasonable compromise with our neighbours a form of apostasy.

Whatever it was, I now see in my rational moments that *For God and Ulster* speaks of the tension in which my Christian life is lived out in this world. The ingrained preference for a particular lifestyle which is the product of my Ulster Protestant upbringing cannot be the final arbiter of my behaviour, for it is often in conflict with my loyalty to Christ. This is the same Christ who said: "Give Caesar what is his, and give God what is his." The motto on the badge now reminds me that it is here, on this space of earth, that Christ's ultimate lordship has to be fleshed out and for such a single purpose I was redeemed.

Edward Donnelly

Edward Donnelly has been a minister in the Reformed Presbyterian Church of Ireland since 1968 with pastorates in Co Antrim, Cyprus and, presently, Trinity Reformed Presbyterian Church in Newtownabbey. He teaches New Testament Language and Literature in the Reformed Theological College, Belfast and is joint-editor of the Reformed Theological Journal. As pastoral commitments permit, he carries on an extensive ministry of preaching and lecturing in various other countries.

I AM, BEFORE EVERYTHING ELSE, A CHRISTIAN. This is my basic identity, conferred by God who has adopted me, through faith in Christ, into His family. I am also an Ulsterman, born and brought up in this province and prejudiced enough to agree with Richard Hayward that it is "the best of all places to live in."

What relationship is there between these two identities? I regard my Ulster background as a singular blessing. I appreciate the religious heritage and commitment to biblical Christianity of this place and the genuine godliness of many Ulster people. I am thankful to be British, part of a nation that has been unusually favoured and used by God. While holding individual Roman Catholics in high regard, I believe that the Roman Catholic system has been responsible for keeping much of this island in spiritual darkness and am glad to have been relatively free of its influence. My faith has been informed and enriched by the circumstances of my background.

Natural patriotism is intensified in the face of threat or perceived injustice. For nearly thirty years the fabric of our society has been torn by terrorists without honour, compassion or anything constructive to contribute. Part of the community has nourished them by a tacit support, wider than is often admitted. The media have been biased and gullible, evidencing little sympathy with or understanding of the wishes of the majority here. These pressures tend to make me protective of Ulster, feeling its pain and wishing to do what I can to defend its integrity.

But that is where the danger lies. National loyalty becomes an idol if we identify our political preferences with the Kingdom of God, our citizenship with our Christianity. We can be reluctant to acknowledge past discrimination in our society. We can refuse to recognise that many of our fellow-citizens have been made to feel outsiders and that, in some respects, we are now reaping what past generations have sown. We can be blind to the defects of an educational system which deprived Ulster Protestants of the riches of their own Irish music, literature and history. We can regard honest self-examination as treachery to the cause.

So I must avoid such sin and have confidence in the power of the gospel and in the sovereign providence of my heavenly Father, who will overrule all things for the benefit of His people, no matter what constitutional developments may take place. My Christian identity is so overwhelmingly more important than earthly citizenship that the two should not be linked. Disregarding more limited loyalties, my primary commitment is to that body in which "there is no Greek or Jew...barbarian, Scythian, slave or free, but Christ is all and is in all" (Colossians 3.11). I am pledged to live for the interests of my Saviour and the spiritual well-being of those around me, and to rejoice that the future is in God's hands.

For God and Ulster? No. 'For Christ and His Kingdom'.

Robin Eames

Robin Eames was born in 1937.

Educated at the Queen's University of

Belfast and Trinity College, Dublin, he

was ordained in the Church of Ireland in

1963 and served in parishes in Bangor,

Gilnahirk, Belfast and Dundela, Belfast.

He was elected Bishop of Derry and

Raphoe in 1975, then Bishop of Down

and Dromore in 1980. He was elected

Archbishop of Armagh in 1986. He

chaired the Archbishop of Canterbury's

Commission on 'Communion and

Women in the Episcopate' in 1988-89.

As well as regular appearances on

television and in the press, he is the

author of a book on the Northern

Ireland situation, Chains to be Broken

(Wiedenfeld & Nicolson, 1992).

He is a member of the House of Lords.

ONE OF THE MOST OBVIOUS MANIFESTATIONS OF sectarianism in certain quarters of Ulster life is the belief that God is on our side. God is our God and all we stand for and all we defend receives some sort of divine preferential treatment. God favours our position, and our vision of the Almighty is of a God who specially favours what we must defend. Therefore what we believe and what we feel we must protect is our version of the truth. Our belief is right, whatever the cost, and what others who have a different view of politics or religion hold dear must therefore be based on a mistaken view of a divine right.

So it goes - and it all stems from the corrosive inheritance of sectarian attitudes and sectarian thinking. It is also the consequence of the widespread belief that Protestantism, from a party political perspective even more than a reformed religious one, is in an unending state of siege. The myriad complexities which result from the overlap of religious identity and party political life have contributed to the confusion which has determined that Ulster's political activity can be viewed, with some historical justification, as purely sectarian.

To be born in a Protestant home means that some form of unionism will greatly influence outlook. To be born in a Roman Catholic home means that the influence will be nationalist or republican. Generalisations these may be, but experience shows their accuracy.

Within the Protestant community the diversification of religious traditions has contributed to the contrast between what many a loyalist views as the unity of Roman Catholicism as compared with his or her own religious denominational family. It is only a short step from that to the perception that Roman Catholicism as a religion is totally identified with the political philosophies of nationalism and republicanism. This view has been cemented of late by the use of such phrases as the 'pan-nationalist front'. On the other side, Roman Catholics usually perceive Protestants in a way that entails total identity with unionism.

Commentators have struggled, largely in vain, to explain the roots of these conflicting perceptions. Historical realities and current experiences of how each community has dealt with the peace process in Northern Ireland have clearly illustrated the parameters of the problem. The conclusion that there is too much religion in Ulster and too little Christianity may be popular in some quarters - it also contains sufficient truth to warrant approval.

The real task for the Christian Church in Northern Ireland is to proclaim the universality of a gospel of love. In so doing it is faced with the harsh realities of sectarian attitudes which have proved so negative and costly down through our history. In facing this challenge, the integrity of separating basic belief in Almighty God from sectional interests is paramount. Identification with the genuine fears and feelings of members of individual denominations is but one part of the sensitive balance. Yet that must never be allowed to blind the Church to its primary task: to proclaim and to witness to the reconciling and forgiving presence of a God for all seasons - and for all the people of this divided community. Ulster needs God - but it needs a God who transcends the barriers.

Brian Ervine

Brian Ervine, a native of East Belfast, is

a teacher at Orangefield High School.

He wrote and produced a magazine

programme about Ulster culture and

history entitled Dalriada *for Belfast*

Community Radio. He has written two

plays - Somme Day Mourning *and*

Haunt of Dragons. *He also writes and*

performs his own songs. He is a

graduate of the Queen's University of

Belfast in both Education and Theology.

THE 'OTHER' IRISH

Ulster Protestants differ as to who they are but are certain who they are not. They are the 'other' Irish.

De Valera and Pearse, taking their cue from nineteenth century nationalism, viewed them as 'a rock in the road' to be blasted out of the way - ethnic cleansing compliments of violent republicanism - or as second-class Irish, or not Irish at all, to be assimilated and stamped with the Gaelic imprimatur - cultural ethnic cleansing which denigrated and patronised their culture.

To some they are merely deluded Irishmen, mesmerised by the twinkling jewels in the British crown, who will one day emerge from their enthralment and realise their true identity; a wayward Paddy - now read Billy - Reilly who will return to the 'the four green fields' of Ballyjamesduff and the outstretched arms of a keening Kathleen Ni Houlihan.

Yet to the Ulster people Kathleen is Medusa whose dread vipers hiss contradictory messages; whose Gorgon stare will petrify and destroy their identity and whose embrace is death itself.

Two nations inhabit the same island. The refusal of one to recognise the other simply exacerbates the conflict.

An Israeli is not a Palestinian; a Serb is not a Croat; neither is a Hutu a Tutsi. When asked to bury their differences the Rwandans and Slavs do - they bury each other, usually in mass graves.

But for the rule of a comparatively benign British dictatorship in Northern Ireland and the presence of thousands of security force personnel the rabid dogs of massacre and obscenity would run completely amok.

The greatest obstacle to any agreement here are those three infernal witches - Hypocrisy, Intolerance and Meanness of Spirit, which could impel Ulster like a tragic Macbeth to wade through a sea of blood.

With its stress on the 'elect of God' motif and emphasis on separation from 'the unclean thing', Ulster Protestantism has developed the self-righteous trait of the Pharisee. The main Unionist parties who refuse to talk to representatives of paramilitaries revere the memory of Carson and Craigavon both of whom gave their unconditional support to Crawford the gunrunner.

Members of a party born out of protest marches and civil disobedience persecute Derry's Unionist mayor for doing likewise. Republicans insist on the principle of consent for Orange marches while failing to subscribe to it at the Dublin Forum and in the Mitchell report. Indeed there has never been consent for their campaign of murder and bombing. The victim becomes the persecutor and still maintains his victimhood.

For two years we have indulged the illusion of peace. A fragile edifice of reconciliation was painstakingly built on the fault line between two political ideologies, the basic assumptions of which were completely contradictory. The tremors of Canary Wharf and Manchester produced the earthquake at Drumcree and created a yawning abyss between the two peoples.

Three paramilitary groupings exist where there was one. Should communal violence restart, a dreadful Nemesis will descend upon the whole island. Republican expectations have been unrealistically heightened and unionist fears fuelled - a recipe for catastrophe unless some *realpolitik* can be injected through dialogue.

Should our respective branches of Christianity and politics fail to bear the fruit of Sincerity, Tolerance and Generosity of Spirit the tree may be chopped down to stoke the fires of sectarian hate.

Roy Garland

Roy Garland was born in Belfast. In the early sixties he studies at All Nations Bible College in London. In the late sixties and early seventies he was a leading officer in Tara, a loyalist paramilitary organisation. During this period he served as a member of the Standing Committee of the Ulster Unionist Council, as an officer on the Ulster Young Unionist Council and as Worshipful Master of Ireland's Heritage LOL No. 1303. In later years he became involved with the Dutch / Northern Ireland Group and the Corrymeela Community. A former Chairman of the New Ireland Group, he rejoined the Ulster Unionist Party after an absence of 20 years. He teaches Sociology, Religion and Politics in Lisburn College. He is the author of The Ulster Volunteer Force Negotiating History (Unpublished MSSc thesis, 1991).

FOR GOD AND ULSTER IS FOR ME AN AMBIVALENT phrase (mis)used to justify intolerance and ethnocentrism (see Roel Kaptein, *Ethnocentrism in Northern Ireland: Its Escalation into Violence and Terrorism*, Unpublished Paper 1992). The latter involves an increasingly insecure and hence aggressive assumption that one's own society, nation, church or whatever, is the measure of all things. *For God and Ulster* is also akin to Emile Durkheim's sacred core that is at the heart of every society and forms the basis of social solidarity. Such gods endow flags and emblems with a sacred quality so that they come to symbolise tribal deities - fearsome gods who reflect and can stimulate violence and discord.

This sacred quality has been identified by Rene Girard as the Janus god of every society. Primitive man had no difficulty conceiving of a god with two heads - one violent, the other life giving. This is not the God and Father of Jesus whose gospel knows no geographical, political, social, gender, national or racial barriers (Galatians 3.23). God in the Bible is the God of the weak and powerless, not the god of power and politics.

Those who preach a political gospel or attempt to shape the gospel into a weapon are perverting it. Jesus spurned violence and in consequence we drove him from our society. Sometimes God in the Old Testament may appear as a violent god but there are frequent glimpses of a "still small voice" (1 Kings 19.12) who desires not sacrifice but mercy (Hosea 6.6). In the New Testament He is the God of light who has no dark side (1 John 1.5). We find Him among prisoners, the sick, the hungry, the naked and strangers (Matthew 25.31-46). This God has a 'bias to the poor' (David Sheppard).

Ulster Volunteer Force men who took *For God and Ulster* as their motto uncovered for me the truth of Matthew 25 - that God meets people in surprising circumstances (Hebrews 13.2). The story of the good Samaritan (Luke 10.33-37) affirms that God is found in unexpected places, among enemies and among those we might despise.

I find it noteworthy that among Jesus' disciples there appears to have been at least one 'paramilitary' Zealot (Matthew 10.4), yet Jesus, despite his rejection of violence, is not on record as having condemned him. Jesus was more concerned with the 'righteous' who are blind to their own hypocrisy (Luke 18.10-14). In the name of God and of the 'nation', the 'righteous' have used the gospel to wound and to win in their power struggles. As a consequence we make each other slaves to guilt, shame and grief. In this sense we become agents of Satan (Mark 8.31-33), causing others to stumble.

For God and Ulster also conveys the reality that faith cannot be divorced from life. Politics should be about the necessary and sometimes mundane activities of everyday life and Christian politicians should serve the whole community. In Northern Ireland, however, politics is a dangerous 'game', often centred upon tribal gods who are confused with the New Testament God of light. Hence Northern Ireland politics involves violent 'religious' struggles in which no compromise is possible. Ulster's god, like all national gods, wounds, denigrates and destroys. This is not the one who, in the midst of great suffering, cried "Father forgive them for they know not what they do" (Luke 23.34).

Will Glendinning

Will Glendinning is Development Officer with the Community Relations Council with responsibility for generating the community relations perspective in a variety of policy areas, including economic development, social services, further education, planning and sport. He is also involved in the development of 'neutral' or 'shared' venues for groups and organisations. Prior to joining CRC in 1990 he worked for Help the Aged. He also worked as Education Officer with the Northern Ireland Council on Alcohol. He was Chair of the Northern Ireland Association of Citizen's Advice Bureaux and is currently on the Board of Community Technical Aid and the British Legion Housing Association. For ten years he served on Belfast City Council as an Alliance Party representative for west Belfast. He now lives in rural County Armagh where he runs a sheep farm.

THOUGH I COME FROM A PROTESTANT AND unionist tradition, my initial reaction to the phrase *For God and Ulster* is to think of a mural on a gable wall and to feel shame, anger, fear and exclusion from the culture that requires such a statement.

Shame, because the narrowness of being *For God and Ulster* means that some are seen as being for neither God nor Ulster and are excluded or exclude themselves - part of another tribe or tradition. Anger, because I abhor the bigotry and prejudice that comes with the phrase and what it results in. Fear that, despite my background, I am not part of that culture and therefore must be an outsider, even a 'traitor' or 'Lundy' or 'turncoat'. Exclusion, because being on the outside means that I do not share in the positive elements of tribal bonding that come from being on the inside - leading sometimes to regret that somehow I am missing out on the solidarity that comes from belonging.

Moving beyond my initial reaction I see that the situation is much more complex. I may not feel I am on the inside but I come from that tradition - I and my family and relations, we are all connected to it. We cannot and should not try to deny our roots. While we may not be full members, neither are we part of the other tradition of Catholic nationalist Ireland. In my time in politics I had the privilege of representing people from both those traditions in west Belfast. That gave me an opportunity, not available to many, to understand the fears, the identities and the hopes of people from those traditions. Mostly, these were people with little power; people suffering from the problems of low income, low esteem, and the viciousness of the violence around them. Perhaps, as a result, I can understand the need for statements like *For God and Ulster* and their nationalist equivalents.

Now I live in rural Armagh along a sectarian interface, seeing things in yet another perspective. Here my neighbours - the people I do business with, who help with my farm, who mind my daughter, people whose kitchens I sit in and chat about the weather and the price of lambs - are members of the Orange or the Black or play in local bands. My daughter's friends learn the accordion or the trumpet in bands that take part in local parades. These are ordinary people, good people - not 'odd-balls' who have arrived from the seventeenth century. They join the Orange and the bands as much for the comradeship as because of any antagonism to the Catholic Church and its teachings. Yet they are seen by those outside as being outdated, bigoted, intransigent; as people who have been duped and misled and who, if they would only see the errors of their ways, would suddenly change and all would be well.

I want the phrase *For God and Ulster* to encompass all the traditions - to be inclusive. Perhaps what I am saying is that I want the space to be part of that other - often unrecognised - tradition, which has been here all along. It is made up of the people who do not want to be put in either box, but who want to celebrate the diversity of our various cultures.

Ken Groves

Ken Groves was born and brought up in a large working class Protestant housing estate in East Belfast. After being involved in various aspects of voluntary work, he studied community youth work at the University of Ulster at Jordanstown. For the past ten years he has been involved in various initiatives in full time youth work. He is currently employed by Frontier Youth Trust, a Christian organisation that supports and resources youth workers working with disadvantaged young people throughout Northern Ireland.

WHAT FOLLOWS IS NOT MEANT TO BE AN attempt at in-depth analysis of the relationship between Christianity and politics or anything else for that matter. It is simply a few personal reflections from someone who grew up in a community in which the statement *For God and Ulster* was very familiar.

Symbols and slogans can become invisible when they form part of our surroundings. We breathe them in each day and they eventually become part of us. Even if we are unsure of how they should be interpreted they are familiar and comfortable. It is only when they are missing or replaced by something else that we realise their significance.

Despite living in a divided society, shared stories and symbols make it possible for people to feel that they can still be part of a community with a strong sense of identity and belonging. Frank Wright in his *Northern Ireland: A Comparative Analysis* (Dublin, 1987) described Northern Ireland as an "ethnic frontier society," a place populated by people who belong to differing and, at times, conflicting traditions. He believed that the use of religious rhetoric tended to obscure the ethnic character of the dispute.

On this point Duncan Morrow notes that "while Catholics in Northern Ireland usually express the problem in national political terms, calling themselves Irish,

FAITH IN ULSTER

Protestant use of religious terminology as a mark of communal identity is in part an attempt to record their differences with Irish nationalists without having to rely on Britain. In effect, the more British nationality and ethnicity is denied, the more Protestantism will be crucial to identity." *Escaping the Bind in Northern Ireland: Teaching and Learning in the Ethnic Frontier* (Jerusalem, 1992).

For God and Ulster means different things to different people but, whatever it means, it always involves powerful emotions. As a youth worker I have come to see how important it is for young people to feel that they belong. This is a basic human need that we all have. Within Northern Ireland these needs can quickly be exploited - the fear of rejection can be a powerful force in determining behaviour. Many acts of savagery have been carried out in the name of God and Ulster and many young lives from both communities have been destroyed. Despite this, our words of condemnation can sound very hollow. We may totally disagree with the rhetoric daubed on gable walls, but at least it is an honest expression of feelings. It may represent something sinister and disturbing, something that is born out of insecurity and fear, but it is real and we need to listen and understand before we offer simplistic solutions and meaningless words of condemnation.

As Morrow says: "Recipes for resolving or interpreting conflict which do not give place to the real experience of all those caught up in the reality of its effects can never fully transcend the conflict. This is the root of the considerable antipathy from those caught up in conflict areas to the easy 'solutions' dreamed up outside the vortex of violence in which the dreamers have no cost to pay in the resolution."

Michael Hall

Michael Hall was born in Belfast in 1949. Since 1968, apart from a two year period when he and his wife went globe-trotting, he has been continuously involved in cross-community activities.

He spent six years as a social worker but resigned after being told to cease the community-orientated approach to social work he had been developing.

Now self-employed as a 'desk-top publisher', he writes and produces Island Pamphlets, *the purpose of which is to facilitate debate at the grassroots and to stimulate awareness among both communities of their shared heritage. He and his wife are founder-parents of Hazelwood Integrated Schools.*

TO ME THE SHIBBOLETH *FOR GOD AND ULSTER!* epitomises the inward-looking and exclusivist attitudes so prevalent on both sides of Northern Ireland's communal divide. It even manages to be doubly exclusive, encompassing both religious belief and national identity.

Many years ago a family friend, troubled by my agnosticism, accosted me thus: "No doubt when you have children they'll be brought up knowing nothing of religion!" "On the contrary," I replied, "when they begin to question I will tell them about Islam, Judaism, Buddhism..." Before I could complete my list he blurted out: "That's not what I mean by 'religion' - I mean Christianity!" Like so many others here - Protestant and Catholic alike - he dismissed the rest of the world's great religions as being of little consequence. Indeed, his conception of 'religion' was even narrower than 'Christianity', for to him God was most certainly a 'Prod'.

Such a limitation is also inherent in the 'Ulster' component of the shibboleth, for it too fails to do justice to the richness of **my** heritage. I love this land, its places of solitude and its people, yet I refuse to define myself as exclusively 'British', 'Irish', or even an 'Ulsterman', as **all** these labels fail to describe the **totality** of my cultural inheritance. For the inheritance I value is not confined to home-grown culture, but includes Ibsen, Rachmaninov, Indian sitar music, Zen poetry,

Islamic art... My heritage is global, one that connects me to cultures far beyond these shores.

Perhaps I might have accepted the label of 'Ulsterman' or 'Irishman' as a necessary starting point if many of those who most vociferously proclaim these identities had not infused them with a narrowness of vision and a meanness of spirit. If to be a 'true Ulsterman' requires that you adopt an irrational anti-Irish mentality, and to be a 'true Irishman' requires that you cling obsessively to an anti-British antagonism, then I want nothing to do with either.

Not long into our present 'Troubles', while involved in cross-community endeavours, I received personal threats not only from those defending 'God and Ulster' but from those fighting for 'Holy Gaelic Ireland', with the consequence that I was spurred to undertake something I had long aspired to: hitch-hike around the world. That experience confirmed what I already knew: that the peoples of our planet, while possessing a rich cultural diversity, could not disguise the commonality of their basic humanity. Whether living with a family in Fiji, or travelling across the Afghan desert in the company of jovial villagers, or being frequently amazed by the hospitality of the Burmese...or the Japanese...or the Nepalese...I felt at **home**. In such circumstances the cry *For God and Ulster!* would have seemed quite meaningless, and quite ridiculous.

I really like living in this land, but I regret having to witness daily the fruits of its narrowness of vision, its territoriality, its bigotry. This society would have so much more to offer its citizens if it transcended *For God and Ulster!* and *Tiocfaidh Ár Lá!* and entered the real world.

David Hewitt

David Hewitt was born in Belfast and educated at the Royal Belfast Academical Institution and the Queen's University of Belfast. A solicitor in Belfast, he is an elder in his local Presbyterian church and Chairman of ECONI, which he co-founded.

I WAS COMFORTABLE WITH THE VALUES OF MY upbringing - middle-class, grammar school, Protestant, conservative evangelical shaped by the pietism of the Plymouth Brethren. Northern Ireland was our country. There was a foreign state across the border. To judge by the poor roads and the people begging in the streets of Dublin, things were not so good down there.

Biblical truths grew in importance and the areas of disagreement between the reformed faith and Roman Catholic teaching were emphasised and repeated. Preachers expounded on Vatican power and intrigue drawing on biblical imagery, producing enough evidence to make it credible to a young mind. Suspicion and distrust were reinforced when, as a young teenager, I travelled south with my team to engage Blackrock College on the rugby field. On a dark, wet, Friday night we were met by a cigarette smoking - and inebriated? - Roman priest and led along corridors, bare except for religious statues.

I was easily persuaded that the real enemy of the Kingdom of God was the Roman Catholic Church. I read avidly the literature of extreme Protestants depicting the worst excesses of Rome during the period of the Reformation. A year spent in correspondence with the Catholic Truth Society confirmed my prejudice - doctrinal error had come to me straight from the horse's mouth.

It was reassuring to witness the 'Twelfth' parades at the bottom of our park as they made their way up the Lisburn Road to the field. Here was strength, not only in numbers, but in dignity, in dark suits and bowler hats, in biblical texts on banners, in the bands playing the 'Hymns of Zion'.

Even as I approached university years my understanding of the issues remained very superficial. 'A' level History focused on Europe and the Commonwealth - Ireland was excluded. There were a few years spent in joint endeavour with hard men from Limerick and Galway on the Irish rugby XV, striving to overcome - particularly the English. Yet this did nothing to weaken my inbred Britishness.

I was settling into practice as a young solicitor in Belfast when the civil rights agitation began. Among the leaders of this rebellious mob were some of my contemporaries at Queen's - not personal friends, they had not been members of the Bible Union or the Rugby Club. My sense of justice was satisfied when they encountered the heavy hand of the law.

Years later, during the hunger strike, I developed a close friendship with two fellow solicitors - ardent nationalists and sincere practising Catholics. From them, and others I met through them, I slowly came to understand and accept that their Irish nationalist aspiration was as noble and valid as my Protestant unionist aspiration. I began to comprehend their deep sense of historical alienation. These were not easy lessons to learn in the midst of the continual onslaught of the IRA. But it was reassuring to know that my nationalist friends were as distressed by terrorist outrages as I was.

Around the same time another personal encounter led to another learning experience. My understanding of Scripture led me to believe that the Kingdom of God was fairly well centred in the evangelical Protestant tradition. But now, through a friend from my own evangelical tradition, I was discovering practising Catholics whose commitment to Jesus Christ and the Scriptures was undeniable. I took opportunities to have fellowship with such people, reluctantly at first. I can only say that these experiences, though culturally uncomfortable to begin with, were immensely liberating.

The lethal mix of national identity, bad religion and exclusive claims to pieces of land has left a legacy that will not quickly be overcome in Ireland. Those who claim to follow Christ have an inescapable obligation to be engaged in the task of making peace and building trust. The credibility of the gospel is at stake.

Finlay Holmes

Finlay Holmes retired in 1996 after teaching Church History for thirty-three years - eight years in Magee Theological College and twenty-five in Union Theological College and the Faculty of Theology of the Queen's University of Belfast. His major interest has been in Presbyterians and politics in Irish history, in particular the correlation of conservatism in theology and politics and radicalism in theology and politics. Among his publications are a biography of Henry Cooke, a history of Irish Presbyterianism and, most recently, a published lecture entitled Presbyterians and Orangeism, 1795-1995 *(Presbyterian Historical Society of Ireland, 1996). He was Moderator of the General Assembly in 1990-1991.*

I CONFESS THAT WHEN I HEAR FOR GOD AND... anything or anyone else alarm bells begin to ring. I cannot forget the First Commandment:

> *I am the Lord your God...You shall have no other gods before me. You shall not make for yourself an idol in the form of anything in heaven above or on the earth beneath or in the waters below. You shall not bow down to them or worship them (Exodus 20.2-5).*

Our loyalty to God is absolute, all other loyalties are relative. In the film Chariots of Fire, Eric Liddell tells the Prince of Wales, who has appealed to him as a patriot to run on Sunday in the Olympic Games and sacrifice his principles, "Sir, God knows I love my country, but that is a sacrifice I cannot make." If patriotism conflicted with God's law, then, for Liddell, God's law came first.

Idolatry did not disappear with the ancient world and there is no more venerable idol than the tribe or nation. Conor Cruise O'Brien warns in *God Land: Reflections on Religion and Nationalism* (Harvard UP, 1988) against the dangers of "holy nationalism," the nadir of which was the holy nationalism of the Third Reich - "The Nation idolizing itself."

For God and Ulster recalls the Ulster Covenant of 1912, in which our forefathers pledged themselves to resist Home Rule as a sacred duty. Some of their critics saw what they were doing as idolatry, an exercise in self-interest, protecting privilege and serving Mammon rather than the God and Father of Jesus Christ. The Irish historian Joseph Lee has suggested that it was "the traditional Presbyterian technique of reminding God whose side He was on"!

Of course our forefathers were well aware of the dangers involved in identifying the cause of unionism with the cause of God. The Presbyterian *Witness,* while acknowledging "the blasphemy" of associating God with one party rather than another, insisted that their opposition to Home Rule was because they believed that it would hinder the advance of the Kingdom of God in Ireland. Thus Protestant Church leaders, including Henry Montgomery, the evangelical Moderator of the General Assembly, signed the Covenant immediately after Carson and Craig.

Whether they were right or wrong in their situation, our situation is different. Britain has changed - its secular ethos is probably more alien to Ulster Protestants than the ethos of the Irish Republic. Vatican II has changed Roman Catholic relationships with Protestants. There are still political, economic, social and personal reasons for preserving the Union with Britain, but it is by no means clear that there are theological reasons. I am sure that many evangelicals in the Irish Republic would contend that there are none.

Herbert Butterfield, in his magisterial study of *Christianity and History* (Cambridge, 1949), suggests that Christians have less reason than others to be afraid of political change, of new kinds of society or civilisation. He argues that "if one wants a permanent rock in life and goes deep enough for it, it is difficult for historical events to shake it." He concludes: "There are times when we can never meet the future with sufficient elasticity of mind, especially if we are locked in the contemporary systems of thought (and even more if we are locked in yesterday's system of thought). We can do worse than remember a principle which both gives us a firm Rock and leaves the maximum elasticity for our minds: the principle: Hold to Christ, and for the rest be totally uncommitted."

For God and Ulster for the Christian must mean that God's will should be done in Ulster, in every area of life.

Mark Houston

Mark Houston was born in 1961 in East Belfast. He worked as a mechanical engineer in the local construction industry before being appointed to the pastorate of City Church, Belfast in 1994. He ministers in the Lower Ormeau / Holy Land area of the city with a particular emphasis on peace and reconciliation and social justice. He is a member of the ECONI Steering Group.

FOR GOD AND ULSTER - A RALLYING CALL which at appointed times throughout the year is resurrected from traditional gable walls and is loudly paraded along well worn routes throughout the country.

It is a constant reminder of earliest childhood memories of family, community and culture which were forever changed at the onset of the 'Troubles'.

Today it remains a battle cry which, along with 'no surrender' and 'our day will come' keeps us chained to the 'not an inch' politics of yesterday. Despite my personal yearning to forge ahead with new ways and new citizenship, it often comes marching along to the sound of drums, clothed in vivid orange and purple, touching something almost primal in my heart.

The grace of God does allow us to walk away from streets with no name and to live where mercy and truth encounter each other and justice and peace kiss. The grace of God will release us from wearing sashes our fathers wore and break the chains of bigotry and prejudice.

We do not have the luxury of sitting back in some perceived state of enlightenment and gloating spiritually, rather we have to press on towards the heart and mind of Christ.

Yet many in our community believe God and Ulster are synonymous, and elevate Ulster to the be all and end all. Many others reject this concept and instead hold up nationalism, socialism or some other 'ism' as their *raison d'être*.

Could it be that God is neither for Ulster nor Ireland, but rather that the character and nature of the Trinity is for a diverse people who are created to think, look and live differently in an attitude of respect and tolerance and, further still, for a people who learn to celebrate the things that make us different.

Could it be?

David Jardine

David Jardine was born in Banbridge. A minister in the Church of Ireland since 1967, he is also a member of the Anglican Society of Saint Francis. As well as parish ministry in St Patrick's on Belfast's Newtownards Road, he served from 1985-88 in two parishes in New York. He also served as Assistant Chaplain at the Queen's University of Belfast and, from 1975 to 1985, as a Chaplain at Crumlin Road Prison. He is currently leader of Divine Healing Ministries, a group he founded to pray for the healing of individuals and the land. In 1991 he initiated a daily time of prayer for Northern Ireland in St Anne's Cathedral to coincide with the beginning of political talks. Since the start of the multi-party talks in 1996 there has been a daily two hour session of prayer for those involved in the negotiations.

I HAVE ALWAYS FELT THAT AS A CHRISTIAN principle this phrase is very dubious. Indeed, for most people who use the phrase in Northern Ireland, allegiance to Ulster is always above allegiance to God. This was true of the vast majority of men to whom I ministered in Crumlin Road prison. Many had committed awful crimes for the sake of Ulster.

Yet I was aware that, even though I would never be involved in that kind of violent crime, all the blame for the community violence did not lie with the men behind bars. Looking into my own life I could see that there was prejudice there. Although I would never have used the phrase *For God and Ulster* to reflect my own principles, often, I have to admit, I reacted emotionally as if Ulster were more important to me than God. Within myself I often reacted strongly to any threat to the Protestant unionist position. I would always have subscribed to the statement of Jesus that no man can serve to masters. However, I would also have to admit that in my emotions, in my reactions, I was far too quick to defend the Protestant unionist point of view and far too quick to point the finger at the limitations of the other section of our community.

Now I believe that these wrong emotional reactions, which often led to wrong words and actions, are something to be repented of and not something to be justified.

I write as one born and bred in Northern Ireland, who loves this country and its people with their strengths and weaknesses and who has prayed a great deal and encouraged others to pray for the healing of this land. However, I also write as one who knows that prayer and conversion of life must go hand in hand. And I am very aware of the need for repentance in my own life first - a repentance that also needs to take place in the churches and wider community in Northern Ireland.

I have been touched by the writings of a Ugandan bishop, Festo Kivengere. In his book, *Revolutionary Love,* he says that for the Christian when a relationship is broken or strained there is a quick way to bring healing - that is to go and apologise for the part that we played in the breaking of the relationship; to apologise first of all to God and, if necessary, to the other person. We are not to go to put that person right or point the finger, but simply to go and apologise on our own behalf. That takes humility; but I believe that it is the way forward for us in Northern Ireland, both as individuals and as communities.

So I confess that I am happier with the phrase *For God and His Glory Alone* than with *For God and Ulster.* I know that I must try to move forward giving my allegiance to God first before any other allegiances and coming humbly to Him in repentance when I fail, to receive His gracious forgiveness. At the same time I will continue working and praying for the healing of this land which I love, which is my home, that His Kingdom may come here and that His will may be done in this part of earth as it is in heaven.

Brian Kennaway

Brian Kennaway was educated at Trinity College, Dublin and Union Theological College, Belfast. He was ordained as a minister of the Presbyterian Church in Ireland in 1976.

He is a Deputy Grand Chaplain of the Grand Orange Lodge of Ireland and Convenor of the Education Committee. In 1995 the Committee published the booklet The Order on Parade. Together with Ian Meredith, he has written The Orange Order: An Evangelical Perspective (1993). He has been a member of Christian Crusaders LOL 1339 since 1964.

TO UNDERSTAND ANY PHRASE OR SLOGAN IT IS necessary to understand the background against which it arose. This is particularly true of this slogan, *For God and Ulster*, which has gripped the imagination of generations of Ulster men and women.

The Context

The historical backdrop against which the slogan arose is European Romanticism. In Germany the 'Faith and Fatherland' slogan united piety and patriotism. William Blake (1757-1827), the first of the great English romantic poets, joined together romanticism and nationality, seen most notably in his hymn *And did those feet...* which affirms:

> *I will not cease from mental fight,*
> *nor shall my sword sleep in my hand,*
> *till we have built Jerusalem*
> *in England's green and pleasant land.*

While Blake in his mystical romanticism appears to equate the Holy City to England, Patrick Pearse (1879-1916), the Irish nationalist, takes things even further by viewing Ireland in her struggle for independence in Messianic terms. He wrote: "The Gaelic League was...a prophet and more than a prophet. But it was not the Messiah...the people itself will perhaps be its own Messiah, the people labouring, scourged, crowned with thorns, agonising and dying, to rise again immortal and impassible." Hence the emotive timing of the 'Easter Rising' to symbolise the 'resurrection' of the nation alongside the 'blood sacrifice'.

This is the historical backdrop of romanticism against which our forefathers coined the phrase *For God and Ulster*. An appreciation of this background will keep us from misunderstanding the content of the slogan.

The Content

Our forefathers were living, not just in a romantic age, but a religious age in which churchgoing and religious observances were part of their environment.

When the slogan *For God and Ulster* was coined by the founding fathers of the Ulster Volunteer Force in 1912 it was an expression of both their religion and their nationality. To them there was no contradiction or confusion in aligning their religious piety with their patriotism.

Moreover, what is evident from the structure of the slogan is that God comes before nationality. The founders of the UVF at the turn of the century saw it as their God given responsibility to do all in their power to retain their allegiance to their national British identity. For them this was the safeguard against 'Rome Rule'. The choice was between freedom or slavery, and they chose to embrace the freedom of British democracy, rather than the slavery of a State dominated by the Roman Catholic Church. Subsequent events over the next seventy-five years and more proved them right.

The Contemporary

The use of the old UVF slogan by contemporary groups only adds to confusion. For many, who have no sense or knowledge of history, the only understanding they have of the slogan *For God and Ulster* is through its use by a paramilitary group.

While there is no copyright on the use of the slogan, those who make use of it should bear in mind the historic sense of both piety and patriotism.

Billy Kennedy

Billy Kennedy is the assistant editor and religious affairs correspondent of the Ulster / Belfast News Letter and the author of two best selling books - The Scots-Irish in the Hills of Tennessee (1995) and The Scots-Irish in the Shenandoah Valley (1996), both published by Causeway Press/Ambassador Productions.

I HOLD THE VIEW THAT RELIGION IS A PRIVATE matter and where a person worships on a Sunday is entirely his or her business. In my case, as an Irish Presbyterian brought up in the Calvinist tradition, I place my faith in a personal relationship with God and in the concept of civil and religious liberty for all. I am a regular attender at my place of worship, but I realise that that this means little when it comes to finding eternal salvation. Occupying a pew for an hour every Sunday may lull some to the mindset of having a spiritual figleaf, but true Christianity only starts at the church door - it continues over the seven days of the week, and the 365 days of the year. Whether I live up to the required standard is entirely up to my God to decide, not those on earth who would piously sit in judgment, but one has got to keep trying to get it right.

The term *For God and Ulster* should mean what it says: the broad mass of people in this province adhering faithfully to the truths of the gospel as proclaimed first by Jesus Christ during his time on earth, then by the Apostles and later expounded by the Protestant Reformers. In this respect, Ulster is no different from any other country in the world in that it needs true Christianity to guide it both spiritually and morally.

Genuine Ulster Protestants sincerely believe that God was their help in ages past in delivering them through various crises which seriously threatened their heritage and culture. The need for God's help has never been more necessary than in today's increasingly secular society and the Protestant and unionist people are certainly not doing Christianity a disservice in seeking spiritual guidance to ensure that their Britishness and their Protestantism is preserved in the most traditional forms on this island. Far better seeking God's help through prayer and devotion than being caught up in the maelstrom of materialism which has sadly beset much of life within Protestant ranks today in many urban localities of our province.

Brought up in a close-knit village community in South Armagh where the church is the cornerstone of the community, I get depressed by the gradual drift away from religion in the inner city of Belfast and in other large towns where the majority of Protestants never darken the doors of a church. Those who talk glibly within the unhealthy confines of a bar room or in situations of sectarian confrontation about being 'a good Protestant' fail miserably to measure up to my criteria of what an Ulster Protestant should stand for.

In my research in the United States on the Ulster-Scots immigrants who settled on the American frontier 200 - 250 years ago I found that God played a central role in their society. The educational prowess they promoted - far above the standards of the day - was largely driven by the Calvinist ethos of the Presbyterian Church. The American constitution was broadly framed from the Presbyterian guidelines on life and democracy. The role of God-fearing Ulster settlers in founding what emerged as the greatest nation on earth was considerable.

Religion and politics have been interwoven in Ulster for centuries and, while there has been a negative side to religious life in this province, church people have by and large been the backbone of decent society here. This applies just as much to the Roman Catholic community as it does to the Protestant community. So the ethos of *For God and Ulster*, while having a particular historical significance for Protestants, is not peculiar to one side of the community in this province.

Michael Longley

*Michael Longley was born in Belfast
and educated at the Royal Belfast
Academical Institution and Trinity
College, Dublin, where he read Classics.
For twenty years he worked for the Arts
Council of Northern Ireland and initiated
the programmes for literature and the
traditional arts and arts-in-education.
His collection* Gorse Fires *(Secker &
Warburg, 1991) won the Whitbread
Prize for Poetry. His most recent
collection* The Ghost Orchid *was
published by Cape in 1995: a Poetry
Book Society Choice, it was also
shortlisted for the T.S. Eliot Prize.*
Tuppenny Stung: Autobiographical
Chapters *was published by Lagan Press
in 1994. He is a Fellow of the Royal
Society of Literature, a member of
Aosdána and a founder member of the
Cultural Traditions Group.*

IT OCCURRED TO ME WHEN I WAS YOUNG THAT God and Ulster might not be too good for each other. The combination seemed to cut out much that I considered normal and acceptable, including myself. My parents came from London to live in Belfast in 1927, and I was born here in 1939. In the streets and the school playground I tuned into Belfast accents, while at home I heard my parents' English voices. From early on social survival required nimble negotiation. I now find dual or even multiple allegiance the only way to proceed. Sometimes I consider myself British, sometimes Irish. Occasionally I lay claim to being an Ulsterman. Most of the time I feel none of these things.

In those early days what did that combination - God and Ulster - exclude? My parents enjoyed a drink - and not just 'a wee mineral'. I felt ashamed when friends discovered a crate of empty Guinness bottles at our back door. "Ach, the English!" I can still hear them muttering. Inside the house there was usually a bottle of gin; and the ashtrays overflowed. I prayed that our sinful home would not be discovered. I knew boys who believed that the Queen of England was heading straight for Hell because she wore nail varnish and attended race meetings. Although my parents were lackadaisical agnostics who never went to church, we 'belonged' to St John's, Malone, where I was baptised and later confirmed. We were Church of Ireland. All of my friends were Presbyterians. They would imitate the Anglican chant and taunt my twin and me: "Sure you might as well be Roman Catholics!"

Dark rumours circulated about the nuns in the convent at the top of the Ormeau Road. In Religious Education classes every effort was made to turn discussion towards the eccentric practices of Catholics - confession, rosaries, the sign of the cross. All of this before the age of ten! My contemporaries were obsessed with Catholics. When a Catholic family moved into our middle class street in South Belfast, the consternation was only partially eased by news that they owned a taxi firm. "Nice people. Plenty of money." A friend's father owned a sheet metal works and, in his spare time, bred bantams. One day, stroking a handsome black cock that perched on the arm of a leather sofa, he told me of a priest who had come to the works. "Looking for gates for his chapel. A lot of my men called him Father. I called him Mister. There's only one Father, and that's our Father in Heaven."

Why do so many Ulster folk believe they have a hotline to God? Their smugness reminds me of the Pharisees who opposed the early Christian movement and with whom Jesus refreshingly disagreed. Our present day Pharisees are so busy clearing out heretics, dismissing the rest of us as blasphemers, that they forget the tender embrace of the New Testament. In conjunction with nationalism (Orange or Green), their fundamentalism (Protestant or Catholic) and their lack of any sense of their own guilt will result in communal disaster. Our churches are to blame for their bigots. Sectarianism takes many subtle as well as crude forms. The fact that our children are still not educated together has little to do with God and everything to do with Ulster. There can be no peace here while sectarian structures and mentalities remain in place. The term Pharisee derives from the Hebrew word meaning, among other things, 'to separate'.

Gordon Lucy

Gordon Lucy was born in Enniskillen and educated at Portora Royal School and the Queen's University of Belfast, graduating with a degree in History. He has experience of teaching, advertising and financial planning. He is a founder member and current Chairman of the Ulster Society, founded with the aim of promoting and preserving the distinctive culture and heritage of the Ulster-British. He is the author of four books including The Local Government Elections of 1993 *(Ulster Society, 1994) and* The Great Convention: The Ulster Unionist Convention of 1892 *(Ulster Society, 1995).*

TO WRITE OF ULSTER POLITICS WITHOUT reference to religion would be akin to describing a barometer without mentioning the mercury. The motto of the original Ulster Volunteer Force is a forceful reminder of the fear that Home Rule would mean 'Rome Rule'. This was a major element in the Ulster Unionist campaign of opposition to the establishment of a Dublin parliament.

In October 1912 the liberal unionist *Northern Whig* opined that "Home Rule is at bottom a war against Protestantism, an attempt to establish a Roman Catholic ascendancy in this country." While some would recoil from such an assessment today, familiarity with the political discourse of that era renders it comparatively easy to comprehend why a liberal newspaper would arrive at such a conclusion. Indeed for many people the history of the twenty six county state, not least Garret Fitzgerald's abortive constitutional crusade and accompanying rhetoric, would suggest that the *Whig*'s assessment was not merely accurate but prophetic.

Contemporaneously with the *Whig* editorial, Dr Maurice Day, the Church of Ireland Bishop of Clogher, observed that "the dividing line [between nationalists and unionists] is essentially a religious one." In similar mode, it is often sweepingly alleged that class is the basis of British party politics and all else is embellishment and detail. Unfortunately,

Dr Day's observation on the nature of Ulster politics is closer to the mark than the class analysis of British politics. Nevertheless, Shane Leslie and Denis Henry respectively are reminders of the existence of Protestant nationalists and Roman Catholic unionists. Protestant nationalists have always been more **visible** than Roman Catholic unionists. However, the latter continue to be a more **numerous** category than the former

While the advent of secularism and the passage of time might have been expected to erode the correlation between religious affiliation and political allegiance, the relationship remains strong.

Professor Marianne Elliott, the biographer of Wolfe Tone and an authority on the United Irishmen, asserted in the *Belfast Telegraph* of 16 August 1993 that "fear of Catholicism, not simply as a religion but as a powerful political system, exists at every level of the Protestant community...it is the main defining element of their Britishness and the perceived link with a Protestant power."

While Professor Elliott's assertion cannot be dismissed out of hand, it is too sweeping, and many Protestants with justice would insist that her observations do not apply to them.

Professor Elliott's assessment of a community of which she is not a member overlooks the importance of culture, identity and orientation. For many, east-west links are of greater importance that north-south links. Indeed, the close proximity of Ulster to Scotland has been a constant factor in shaping and moulding the history of the province. For many Ulster people their culture does not find expression in Irish traditional music, the Irish language or Gaelic games. Their culture and identity is British and, for a great many Ulster people, a specifically Scottish expression of Britishness, whether it be the music of the pipes, the poetry of Burns or Scottish country dancing, let alone a religio-political or intellectual *mentalité*.

While it would be preposterous to disregard the importance of religion, which for many people is of paramount importance, it is appropriate to acknowledge that religious labels are frequently applied to people who are not engaged in a jihad but who are subject to a complex "clash of ethno-national, cultural, religious and political identities."

Roy Magee

Roy Magee was born in 1930. He studied at Trinity College, Dublin and in the United States. Ordained in the Presbyterian Church in Ireland, he ministered in Mersey Street, Belfast, Donacloney, Sinclair Seamen's, Belfast, First Saintfield and Dundonald. He retired in 1995. In recent years he has played a key role in encouraging Loyalist groups to call a ceasefire and to move from violence to a political agenda.

WHEN A PROMINENT TEACHER OF THE LAW asked the Lord Jesus Christ a very pointed and difficult question concerning the greatest and most important commandment, the angels must have paused and leaned over the parapet of heaven to hear which of the 3,600 commandments in the Jewish Law the master was going to pick. Without hesitation He replied, "'Love the Lord your God with all your heart...' This is the first and greatest command." But then He went on, "And the second is like it: 'Love your neighbour as yourself'" (Matthew 22.34-40).

It is interesting that even though the Hebrew people were full of national pride and held the promised land in the highest possible esteem the Lord Jesus made no reference whatever to love for their nation. This is not to say that nationalism was not to be an important aspect of their lives, but rather that their priority was to be God and then neighbours.

Why, when the lawyer asked for the **one** greatest commandment, did Jesus reply by giving him a second? It is surely that He is saying that our love for God is manifested in our love for others. Perhaps realising the sheer bigotry which can be engendered by an individual's national fanaticism, the Saviour emphasises the commandment that we must treat others on an equal footing with ourselves and always on the basis of 'love'. Thus the Jew whose slogan might have been *For God and Israel* would be going contrary not only to the mind and will of God but also to the express teaching of the Messiah.

And yet a similar phrase has become part of the cultural heritage of many Protestant people in Northern Ireland. Perhaps we need to address the question, What do we mean when we chant the slogan *For God and Ulster?* To put both on a par is unquestionably idolatry, but to use the phrase to indicate our priorities is permissible.

For example, if I were to say *For God and Ulster* I would be indicating that my over-ruling commitment is to Almighty God and whatever else I might add following the *and* is simply confirming that I am committed to that in a godly manner and that my attitude to it will always and ever be on the principles of God and His Word. This in effect means that if I am really for God I will never use or display methods of violence, injustice or hatred in my attitude or my speech. Further, it means my relationships with others will be always and only in accord with the way the Lord Jesus Christ lived and spoke - and that takes me apart and challenges every facet of my life.

One of the salient truths taught in Scripture is that God does not make any distinctions. "He deeply loved the world," and whether that be Ulster, the United States of America, Brazil or the Republic of Ireland, He sent His Son to die for the "whosoever" regardless of the nation in which they may live.

Ian Major

Ian Major is a missionary pastor to prisoners in Northern Ireland. He has been involved in prison ministry since 1980 working full time since 1991. He has contributed articles on the Ulster situation to the Belfast Telegraph and the Evangelical Times and has spoken at the Forum for Peace and Reconciliation in Dublin, and ECONI's Christian Citizenship Forum in Belfast.

THE PHRASE *FOR GOD AND ULSTER* HAS STRONG emotive connotations for me. The reasons for that are complex, some shared with most Ulstermen but others distinctive to my evangelical Baptist position.

In common with many of my fellow-countrymen in Ulster, I regard myself as an Ulsterman first, British second and finally - in a strictly geographical sense - Irish. That expression of national identity is an historic one. Ulster nationalism came to self-awareness during - and due to - the Home Rule crisis at the turn of the century. Those who had been happy to think of themselves as British **and** Irish were forced by the British and Irish either to become solely Irish or to rebel against the British and go their own way. My forefathers chose the latter and asserted the right of their Ulster-Scots nationality above that of the British Union of nations. Their right to national self-determination did not depend on the whim of the English, Scots, Welsh or, indeed, the Gaelic Irish. Using the motto *For God and Ulster* my forefathers united to keep their nation free from political and religious tyranny. Today, I stand in their place with those same noble desires, knowing that history - in the sectarian record of the Irish state - has vindicated their assessment of Irish nationalism.

Ulster people today, however, face a changed Irish state and the nationalism it represents. In the course of these present Troubles it seems to have become evident to many Irish nationalists that the Ulster people are not the "Quisling Irish" that Sean McBride so contemptuously labelled us. Now we are to be accorded respect as a separate people, a people whose consent is required if they are to merge with the Irish on this island. Such an enlightened outlook is still in a fragile, infant form and the threat of reversion to One Nation - One Fatherland thinking is very real. Indeed, traditional nationalism / republicanism still holds sway not only among the Provisional IRA but also in important sections of constitutional nationalism in the South. It is therefore crucial that the Ulster people keep a clear vision of their identity and that we articulate that vision accurately in our dialogue with our fellow-countrymen. To do less risks our opponents miscalling our responses to their overtures, where 'persuasion' may be perceived as 'coercion' and resisted.

From my Baptist perspective, I am concerned that the *For God* section of this motto has been misconstrued by many to imply that our struggle for national rights is of itself a spiritual conflict - as if the people of Ulster are identical to the people of God, that Ulster's cause and the gospel's are the same. The truth is that every nation stands in the same relationship with God as does Ulster. All nations exist at His discretion and are answerable to His judgment for their unrighteous acts. The liberties we claim for Ulster belong to every nation, and it is our duty to make every effort to reach a just settlement with our neighbours who claim Irish nationality. *For God* can only properly mean that we as a people acknowledge God's sovereign rule over men, and that our regard for Ulster is not in opposition to His rights to our supreme love. *For God and Ulster* is, therefore, to me a valid expression of my role as a Christian citizen.

Bill Malcolmson

Bill Malcolmson is a minister in the Congregational Reformed Church, East Belfast, having previously ministered at the Cliftonpark and Albertbridge Churches, both in Belfast. He is a Chaplain in both the Orange and Royal Black Institutions, Chairman of the Stedfast Association of the Boys' Brigade in Northern Ireland, and Vice-President of the Evangelical Protestant Society.

THESE WORDS, FOR GOD AND ULSTER, SEND ME back immediately in memory to those young men, the flower of this country, who bled and died at the Somme in 1916 to preserve the liberty of this and other nations. They were, in the main, the men of Lord Carson's Ulster Volunteer Force who opposed Home Rule for Ireland in 1912, knowing that Home Rule meant 'Rome Rule'. Their motto was *For God and Ulster* and with that sentiment deeply implanted in their hearts and minds they died in their thousands to maintain our British way of life against any force that would try to take away our civil and religious liberty. The loyal and law-abiding majority population of Ulster will never forget them.

Looking at the phrase *For God and Ulster* today, I firmly believe that here we have a motto well worth following. The inept British Governments of the last twenty seven years have, in the main, forgotten the God of the Bible, and here lies the root cause of our troubles as a nation right across the political and social spectrums. Successive administrations have failed to complete their God-appointed task in protecting the people of Ulster from the expertly organised terrorism emanating from the Republic of Ireland. They have added insult to injury by meeting these terrorists in secret, and by entering into the Anglo-Irish Agreement of 1985 with a hostile nation on our own doorstep, which lays illegal claim upon this part of the United Kingdom. God and righteousness have been set aside conveniently.

The only way back from our present dreadful position is to return to the God of our fathers. Christ said

Seek ye first the Kingdom of God,
and His righteousness, and all other
things shall be added unto you (Matthew 6.33).

As the motto indicates, the first priority today is to promote the Kingdom of God. This can only be accomplished by the preaching and teaching of the Protestant, evangelical and reformed faith, as enshrined in the great confessions coming out of the Protestant Reformation. Such preaching and teaching is necessary to counteract the many false religions and ideologies by which we are surrounded. It would create a healthy spiritual atmosphere, opening the way for a return to high moral standards. We must never forget that "righteousness exalts a nation, but sin is a reproach to any people" (Proverbs 14.34).

This motto puts God first, and we must follow it.

In divine providence God has put men into nations. He has given the nations the moral law summarised in the ten commandments, and has instituted governments to promote righteousness, to execute judgment, to uphold justice, to protect citizens and to punish evil-doers. His elect people are in every nation and therefore He is concerned about the cause of righteousness and truth everywhere. We desire our own British Government to follow this course set by God, and to do so in Ulster. We are all called to be loyal and law-abiding citizens of the land in which we live, and by the very instincts of our nature we love our native soil. By applying the teachings of sound biblical Christianity we would become better citizens and this would have the effect of bringing to Ulster, not man's peace, but God's peace in Jesus Christ our Lord.

The motto *For God and Ulster*, applied in the right spirit, would have a transforming influence for good in this province, and beyond. This motto, which seems to trouble others, has no problems for me.

David McConaghie

David McConaghie is Pastor of Maghaberry Elim Pentecostal Church and Secretary of the Religious Affairs Committee of the Independent Loyal Orange Order.

THE PHRASE *FOR GOD AND ULSTER*, WHILE NOT one I normally use to describe myself and my faith, is nevertheless one I have no difficulties with since it expresses two basic truths I wholeheartedly accept and which I believe all true Christians should practice.

It has in effect two constituent parts, namely, *For God* and *For Ulster*.

As an evangelical Protestant I am indeed for God. Born into a Presbyterian family, I realised in my teens that neither baptism nor any other rite or ceremony could impart saving grace to the soul. Thus, for all my religious background and heritage I was as lost as any man could be. However, by simply trusting in Christ alone as my Lord and Saviour I found peace with God and rest and liberty for my soul. This is the God I am for - not the vague idea of a supreme being, but God as He is exclusively revealed in the Bible. Believing the Bible to be inspired and preserved and hence inerrant, I am for the entire biblical revelation of God and His will. It is then the case that because of the divine origin and miraculous preservation of the Bible I must also consider all religious observance which is contrary to this to be false and therefore against God.

To be for God, then, involves being for the teachings of the Scriptures and against all false religions and philosophies. In the context of Ulster this means that I am against Roman

Catholicism which I consider an idolatrous and blasphemous religion - the largest false religious movement here. Roman Catholicism I believe to be openly hostile to God and His will throughout the entire fabric of its being.

I also consider myself to be for Ulster.

When we remember that Christians are called to be good citizens it is only right that we be good citizens here, seeking to make Ulster as prosperous and righteous as possible. Furthermore, Ulster as part the United Kingdom has shared in the benefits of the Williamite revolution and settlement. As a consequence it has a history and heritage of reformation and revival. This is in sharp contrast to the Irish Republic which rests upon a Roman Catholic foundation whose crowning glories are Knock, Croaghpatrick and Lough Derg. Rome, the sworn enemy of civil and religious liberties, exists primarily for the accruement of political power, and works to subvert and overthrow all obstacles to that.

As a Bible believing Protestant I am for Ulster. I am for the maintaining of civil and religious liberty for all. I am against the stealing away of Ulster's gospel heritage. I am for her continued enjoyment of her God-given blessings which are protected in the United Kingdom, but which are at best only tolerated where Rome's influence is felt.

On these terms I gladly take to myself the label *For God and Ulster*.

Billy Mitchell

Billy Mitchell was brought up in the evangelical tradition but moved to a more secular Protestantism in his teens. He rediscovered the spiritual component of Protestantism while serving a life sentence for activities carried out in furtherance of the cause of the Ulster Volunteer Force and resigned from that organisation while in prison. Since his release on licence in 1990 he has been worshipping with the Church of the Nazarene in Carrickfergus and has been heavily involved in inter-community development work in the North Belfast area. He is a member of the Progressive Unionist Party and regards himself as a Christian Socialist.

EVEN THOUGH I AM A COMMITTED CHRISTIAN and a Progressive Unionist I do not feel that the phrase *For God and Ulster* is appropriate as an expression of my cultural identity. While I fully endorse the view that Christian ethics as mediated through the Word of God ought to inform and influence me in my political and cultural activity, I believe that any philosophy which seeks to legitimise a political or cultural cause by invoking the name of God is bordering on the blasphemous. The love, mercy and grace of God transcend party politics and cultural traditions. God is no less the God of the citizen who aspires to a united Ireland than He is the God of the citizen who aspires to the maintenance of the Union with Great Britain. Ulster Protestants must be careful that they are not guilty of creating a god in their own image.

My identity as an Ulster Protestant has been heavily influenced by inherited attitudes that have been handed down from generation to generation through customs, laws, institutions and family histories. While it is true to say that my identity is derived from my distant Scottish Presbyterian forebears it is also true that it has been constantly modified by the social, cultural and economic influences of the more recent past and of the present. Identity is subject to change. It is not a static thing that is locked in the past but something that is being constantly defined and redefined by different generations in the process of history. There have been times when my Presbyterian forebears have been staunchly anti-English, anti-establishment, pro-Irish and extremely radical in theology. Since the turn of the century my family circle have become progressively pro-British, pro-establishment and conservative in theology. For many of them evangelical Protestantism has become the heartbeat of unionism and it is this blend of evangelical religion and political philosophy that tended to justify their acceptance of the phrase *For God and Ulster* as a summary of their identity.

The past twenty-five years of conflict and violence, coupled with the development of a hostile and aggressive pan-nationalist alliance, have confirmed me in my support for the Union and, while it has not alienated me altogether from a sense of Irishness, the politicisation of a common Irish culture by pan-nationalism has left me extremely uncomfortable with it. My support for the Union is an expression of my desire to remain a citizen of the United Kingdom and of my affinity with the British way of life. I see no contradiction in being both Irish and British just as I see no contradiction in a person being both Scottish and British or English and British.

Unionism for me is a valid political philosophy that should promote the merits of the British way of life for all people, not just for those who are of the Protestant religion. While I have no objection to politics being influenced by Christian ethics I am absolutely opposed to the idea that any party and, more importantly, any government should be controlled by any particular religious denomination. I am committed to the establishment of a new principled pluralist society for Ulster, within the United Kingdom, where each citizen is valued for his or her worth as an individual human being and not on account of his or her religious beliefs.

James Molyneaux

Sir James Molyneaux was born in 1920. From 1941 to 1946 he served in the Royal Air Force. First elected to Parliament in 1970, he has been MP for the Lagan Valley constituency since 1983. He led the Ulster Unionist Parliamentary Party from 1974 to 1995 and was overall leader from 1979 to 1995. Born in the Parish of Killead, he has been a member of the choir of St Catherine's Church since 1930, has served on the Select Vestry for some 50 years and is a member of the Diocesan Council of Connor. He is Sovereign Commonwealth Grand Master of the Royal Black Institution.

FOR GOD AND ULSTER IS ONE OF THOSE IDIOMS which need to be set in perspective. Primeval man placed the yearning for a pagan deity second only to hunger for food. The imaginary demands of the god became the guiding principles for the race or the tribe.

By Old Testament times the authority of the one true God was firmly established and passed down through the priesthood which would be expected to give the seal of Divine approval to the lay head of the nation. We read in First Kings that Zadok the priest anointed Solomon as king over Israel, "and all the people shouted and said, God save the King" (1 Kings 1.39).

With variations, that acclamation of approval has continued through two thousand years of Christian history. Recently, the newly elected President of Russia was blessed in words not very different from those of Zadok the priest. Across the Atlantic, aspiring Presidential candidates raise electors to fever pitch with the cry of 'God Bless America'.

Against this background the phrase *For God and Ulster* can be seen as a blending of the spiritual and the secular. If some utter it as a figure of speech are they any different from all those earlier examples? And who is to judge the sincerity of the owner of the tongue?

The blending of the spiritual and the secular can be seen at the beginning of every day's sitting in the House of Commons. The

Speaker's Chaplain leads Members in the prayer, "Almighty God, by whom alone Kings reign and Princes decree justice, and from whom alone cometh all counsel, wisdom and understanding...."

However, in Britain we now see a campaign to sever the link between Church and State. Aside from the constitutional impact, the danger is that the severance would send the wrong signal - a signal that true religion had been abolished and that the spiritual and secular estates had been disconnected.

There would not be a vacuum, for the void would be speedily filled by secular liberal humanism and there would be created a new world where it would be obligatory to observe a politically correct attitude of neutrality between right and wrong. In such a society it would be useless to argue that conscience would preserve a balance - the 'new agers' would see to that.

So even if the cry *For God and Ulster* has been devalued by some it remains an 'ancient landmark'. Even if some others complain that the terminology is 'not with it' it is still more valuable than confused babble.

Philip Orr

Philip Orr was born in rural County Down. After studying English Literature at the University of East Anglia and the University of Ulster he became a teacher. He has taught at Friend's School, Lisburn and Down High School. He is the author of The Road to the Somme: Men of the Ulster Division Tell Their Story *(Blackstaff, 1987), a study of the 36th Ulster division and its mythology.*

IN 1915, WEARING THEIR ULSTER VOLUNTEER motto *For God and Ulster*, the men of the 36th Division marched onto the troop ships that would take them to the Western Front. In so doing, they joined millions of other young men from all across the world, whose sense of faith and fatherland meant soldiering, sacrifice and possible obliteration.

My own quest to find the grave of a great uncle killed with just such a motto on his badge took me to a neat green graveyard in France in 1988. I was accompanied by a German friend whose own grandfather had also been at the Somme in 1916, firing high explosive shells in my great uncle's direction. While I laid flowers at my chosen headstone in the British section of the graveyard, my friend walked between the rows of German graves in the 'enemy' section of the same small plot of ground - stopping longest where those gravestones were marked by a Star of David, indicating the last resting place of a German Jew who had died for the Reich.

My subsequent travels, friendships and reading have acquainted me with Great War graveyards all over the world - from Turkey to Tanzania. These indicate how world-wide was the grim, magnetic pull of that most criminally futile of all military conflicts - a war fought by European powers bloated by belligerent, imperial self-confidence, achieved at the expense of the indigenous peoples of Asia,

Africa and the Pacific during the previous century.

For God and Ulster - or its synonym in a hundred other languages - was an obligation that led many into the sights of machine-gunners in that distant war.

On a more recent visit to a former Royal Air Force Bomber Command base on the empty levels of the Lincolnshire countryside, I made my way round the exhibitions of photographs and memorabilia. These were displayed in a vast hangar dominated by the black body of a surviving Lancaster bomber.

Mesmerised, excited, taken back to my boyhood war-comics, I found myself suddenly stilled in front of an aerial photograph of Frankfurt being pounded to burning rubble in 1945. Recalling stories told by my German friends, I knew that down there, in bunkers beneath ground, men, women and children would have been shaking and suffocating. In front of that photograph, I stood on either side of a line decreed by enmity.

Am I for God? Yes. **For** His Love, His Grace, His Power to reconcile Mercy and Justice - in Ulster and everywhere else.

For God and Ulster may be where I started from, but it is not where I have ended up.

Norman Porter

Norman Porter was born in Belfast in 1952 and educated at Methodist College, Belfast. In 1970 he and his family emigrated to Australia where he graduated with a BA in Politics from Flinders University. After being awarded a DPhil in Politics from the University of Oxford he returned to Flinders as a lecturer. In 1994 he moved back to Belfast. He is a member of the Ulster Unionist Party and is the author of Rethinking Unionism: An Alternative Vision for Northern Ireland (Blackstaff Press, 1996).

THE PHRASE *FOR GOD AND ULSTER* MAKES ME twitch, if not cringe. It brings back memories of when I once took the phrase to capture a self-evident truth: God, if not Himself Protestant, was certainly on the side of Protestants everywhere and of Protestants in Northern Ireland in particular. Accordingly, the political task of keeping Ulster Protestant and, by extension, of opposing all things Catholic and Irish enjoyed divine favour. Or so it seemed to me. In my case, it wasn't so much that I saw defending Ulster as part of a religious crusade, though I had no quibbles with those who did; it was more that I derived reassurance and a sense of self-righteousness from the convenient assumption that God approved of the Protestant cause in Ulster.

These memories are unsettling. *For God and Ulster* now appears to me as a disturbingly misguided slogan, which is why I twitch and cringe when reminded of how I once thought otherwise. I no longer think, for example, that it is legitimate to invoke God to underwrite one set of interests in a dispute in Irish politics. A New Testament understanding of the Kingdom of God cautions against identifying the cause of God with any parochial political cause. On strictly theological grounds, it seems unduly presumptuous not to plead agnosticism on the question of where God stands in arguments over the constitutional future of Northern Ireland.

To plead more than agnosticism here, as the slogan *For God and Ulster* manifestly does, encourages an intransigent, intolerant spirit which serves to harden political attitudes in a deeply divided society. To base political action on the assumption that Protestantism in Ulster has a unique divine warrant makes it very difficult to recognise the political entitlements of non-Protestants. It virtually forecloses the possibility of meaningful dialogue with nationalists and so deepens the misunderstanding and mistrust that characterise relations between Northern Ireland's two major communities.

For God and Ulster, then, is a slogan that we would be better off without, theologically and politically. To continue to insist upon it is to add to the tragedy of Northern Ireland today. And this, it seems to me, is not only lamentable, but ultimately inexcusable.

Paul Reid

Paul Reid is the leader of Christian Fellowship Church, Belfast and also leads 'Frontline' - an apostolic team committed to church planting in Ireland and around the world. His beginnings in the Brethren have given him a deep love of Scripture and this, coupled with a dramatic experience of the Holy Spirit, transformed his life and ministry. He has a desire to see the current refreshing / renewal move to revival and change Ireland and the nations. He is the author of A New Easter Rising *(Logikos Christian Publishing, 1993).*

THE BIBLICAL CONCEPT OF GOD AND COUNTRY is one routed deep in the Old Testament. The link between Israel and the 'promised land' begins with God's promise to Abram in Genesis 12.1. This is followed up on numerous occasions by God restating that promise to his people (Genesis 15.7; Exodus 3.17; Joshua 1.1-9).

The blessing upon the people was conditional on them being in the right land. That is why so much of Joshua is taken up with getting the 'wrong people' - that is, the Canaanites, Amorites and so on - out of the land. The covenant God made involved three specific clauses - they had to do with property (the land), people (the nation) and prosperity (the blessing). This history of Israel is the history of keeping property, people and the promise of prosperity together.

When the Protestant settlers came to Ulster in the seventeenth century, the history of Israel was much in their mind and reasoning. After years of allegorical interpretation of Scripture, the Reformation brought fresh insight into the Bible with a strong literal form of interpretation. The settlers saw the land of Ulster as 'the promised land', the native Irish as the Canaanites and Amorites. Therefore, the resultant killings of Catholics and theft of their land were justified on very dubious biblical grounds. The story of Israel was transposed to seventeenth century

FAITH IN ULSTER

Ulster and the concept of God, country and blessing became part of our history.

To be for Ulster is to be for God, and as this country is God's gift to the Protestant people, we have a divine right to 'hold what we have' - or so the reasoning goes. But if the principle of interpretation is wrong then the link between God and Ulster is also spurious. We are not an antitype of ancient Israel and those who belong to Christ must surely make the distinction clear. So closely has God's name been linked with the land it appears that God and Ulster have equal billing! For many in the body of Christ the day is fast approaching when a choice will have to be made - not *For God **and** Ulster* but *For God **or** Ulster*.

I am an Ulsterman, I am proud to be Irish and an Ulsterman. I cannot change the past, history or how I was brought up; but my identity and security are not bound up with where I was born. That can only be found in Christ. My ultimate allegiance is to Him alone and to link God's name with Ulster in the way that many in this province have done is to drag that name in the mud. It excludes from God's love and family those who are not of the unionist or Protestant ascendancy. The question is being asked, Just who has our ultimate loyalty, God or Ulster?

John Robb

John Robb is a former Consultant Surgeon. He is a Fellow of the Royal College of Surgeons of England and Ireland and a member of the Senate of the Queen's University of Belfast. In the seventies he helped found the New Ireland Movement and, in 1981, the New Ireland Group. He has written a number of political pamphlets, including 'New Ireland: Sell Out or Opportunity' (1972) and 'Democratic Accountability in a District Health Service' (1992). From 1982 to 1989 he sat in Seanad Eireann (Irish Senate). He has made written and oral submissions to the New Ireland Forum, the Devolution Committee of the Northern Ireland Assembly, the Opsahl Commission and the Forum for Peace and Reconciliation.

WE AFFIRM THE HUMAN RIGHTS OF EVERY PERSON on the planet and these are enshrined in Charters, Declarations, Conventions and Covenants. Yet we are poised for self-destruction through nuclear holocaust or ecological collapse! Something has gone seriously wrong with our calculations.

Another contradiction: we are asked to take responsibility for our actions yet we are called to believe in an infinitely powerful controlling Creator. Before such infinite power are we not infinitely powerless? Where does that leave choice and the will to exercise it? Choice, leading to affirmation or denial of what feels right in conscience, is a means - if not the means - of personal growth or personal atrophy. The question then arises, Is freedom of choice consonant with the will of God?

Perhaps, then, God should be internalised rather than externalised - a power, or better, a reality within us and shared between us rather than a force over us. If positive orientation moves us towards the Christ like state of absolute truth and negative orientation moves us in the opposite direction, then it is possible to conceive of God as the 'gift of capacity' - the capacity to move towards spiritual enlightenment and ultimate atonement or, alternatively, towards spiritual decline and ultimate isolation.

In searching for understanding, the question was put as to why God could not be both internal and external and, by extension, eternal. In a sense the first four words of the Bible - "In the beginning God" - seem to encapsulate such an understanding as the meaning behind the reason, feeling and mystery of life's search. To this statement a little boy responded, "What then was before the beginning!" The only reply that came to mind was, "The real beginning." If God and the beginning are synonymous, all else would seem to flow from that.

When we are untruthful to ourselves or hurtful to others we suffer. Internal disharmony leads to external discord. *For God and Ulster* is an exclusive affirmation. If God is on our side then, by implication, God help everyone else! If, however, God is inclusive of the whole, then the difference which keeps us apart can be transcended through awareness of God. Too often *For God and Ulster* has been used, especially in the past, to identify with the exclusive loyalty of one community only; it alienates one from the other.

This most alienating of centuries has highlighted and created great splits within ourselves and between ourselves, and has obscured the path down which we must travel to find ourselves again. Unless through reflection, through meditation, in retreat and by prayer we are first in touch with ourselves, we will find it difficult to reach out convincingly to the other. In returning to the centre we become aware of the split in the centre and the need for healing.

From the healed centre we reach out to engage, to touch and to embrace - all. This surely is God in Ulster, in Ireland and beyond.

Patrick Roche

Patrick Roche studied Economics and Politics at Trinity College, Dublin and Philosophy at the University of Durham. Recently retired from lecturing in Economics at the University of Ulster at Jordanstown he currently teaches Philosophy of Religion at the Irish Baptist College. He is joint editor with Brian Barton of two books - The Northern Ireland Question: Myth and Reality (Avebury, 1991) and The Northern Ireland Question: Perspectives and Policies (Avebury, 1994). He is the author with Esmond Birnie of An Economics Lesson for Irish Nationalists and Republicans (Ulster Unionist Information Institute, 1995) arguing the economic case for the Union. He is a member of the Cadogan Group and an advisor to the United Kingdom Unionist Party at the multi-party talks.

THE IDENTIFICATION OF UNIONISM WITH A *FOR God and Ulster* mentality makes unionism an easy target as a form of political sectarianism. Proponents of this presentation of unionism explain the 'bigotry' and 'intransigence' characteristic of what they take to be the supremacist mentality of unionists in terms of this sectarianism. At this point the *For God and Ulster* understanding of unionism joins with more secular presentations when, for example, John Hume speaks of the 'Afrikaaner mindset' of unionists, thus identifying unionism with a supremacist mentality understood in terms of racism.

The sectarian and supremacist mentality attributed to unionists is used to explain the claimed discrimination against Catholics which produced what nationalists refer to as the 'nationalist nightmare' in Northern Ireland. This 'nationalist nightmare' in turn is understood to have given rise to a Catholic 'alienation' sufficient to have sustained 25 years of IRA terrorism. At this point the nationalist understanding completes a moral circle. The victims of IRA terrorism become ultimately responsible for its perpetration with the tacit implication that the actual perpetrators are not really morally culpable.

The understanding of unionism as a politics of sectarianism exemplifies a failure to liberate the understanding of unionism and the politics of Northern Ireland from nationalist mythology and stereotype. The 'nationalist nightmare' is based on nothing more substantial than gross exaggeration, as a growing body of research suggests. It is a myth required by the ideology of Irish nationalism to sustain the understanding that Northern Ireland is a 'failed political entity' and to justify the violence used to end partition.

But this suggests that what fundamentally gives plausibility to nationalist complaint - the identification of unionism with sectarianism - may itself be open to dispute. This is indeed the case. Unionism is in fact a form of what in contemporary jargon is designated 'civic nationalism' - that is, an understanding of the nation as a community characterised by equal citizenship and united by a shared set of political practices and values. The substance of civic nationalism was articulated by the signatories of the Solemn League and Covenant of 1912 in their commitment to "the cherished position of equal citizenship within the United Kingdom." But the fact that unionism is a form of civic nationalism means that religious commitment is not essential to unionism - either for the determination of the political identity of unionists or for their refusal to be coerced or cajoled into a united Ireland.

It is precisely at this point that unionism **differs** from Irish nationalism. Irish nationalism is a form of 'ethnic nationalism' in which primary loyalty is to the nation identified in terms of ethnic characteristics such as race, language and religion - which in the case of Irish nationalism is Roman Catholicism. This means that Irish nationalism - in contradistinction to unionism - is inherently sectarian.

This sectarianism, which lies at the heart of Irish nationalism, was significantly nurtured and sustained by an ideologically determined account of Irish history traditionally taught in Roman Catholic schools in Ireland. The outcome has been for Irish nationalists an implacable hostility to the very existence of Northern Ireland and a moral ambivalence towards republican terrorism. This moral ambivalence is not absent from the Roman Catholic Church in Ireland and certainly underpins the *realpolitik* of the Hume-Adams 'peace process'. For republicans, sectarianism sustains the hatred to which the psychology of terrorism ultimately reduces and without which no normal human being could perform the concrete terrorist deed.

The time is long overdue for nationalists to turn away from self-justification in terms of stereotypes of unionism and to confront authentically the realities within their ideology and their psyche which have sustained a quarter of a century of terrorism. The outcome just might be a moral liberation which would deliver peace in Ireland.

John Ross

John Ross is a minister of the Presbyterian Church in Ireland. Ordained in 1960 in Rosemary Church, Belfast, he served as a missionary in Malawi before pastorates in Clough and Seaforde, Dundonald and Holywood. He has been involved throughout his ministry with the world mission of the Presbyterian Church. From 1986 to 1993 he was Convenor of the Church's Race Relations Committee. In 1995 he served as Moderator of the General Assembly. He enjoys travel at home and abroad, recently visiting the USA, India and Nepal in various capacities.

I WAS BORN IN BALLYMENA IN 1936 AND SPENT the formative years of my life there. My childhood years were years of war which may have given me a consciousness of being British.

I grew up in a home where my parents were devout Christians and Protestants. My father was deeply involved in the work of a local church as elder, Sunday School teacher and captain of the Boys' Brigade. He was also an Orangeman - Chaplain and Past Master. My father was a very peace loving person, respectful of other people and highly respected in the whole community. I imbibed much of my upbringing, though I did not follow him into the Order. No pressure was brought on me to join, though good humoured comments were passed about how nice it would be to have a 'Rev. Bro.' in the ranks. Neither I nor any of my peers joined. I could not see membership as having any bearing on my calling to the ministry.

Education for the ministry over a period of years in Derry, Dublin, Edinburgh and Belfast, experiences in Africa during a period of enormous change, and deepening understanding of Scripture did not make me value any less my upbringing as an Ulster Protestant or my more specific Presbyterian Ulster-Scots roots, but it did enable me to look more critically at my identity.

What did *For God and Ulster* mean for me? It became a phrase with which I could not identify as I saw the false assumptions that lay behind it and the contexts in which it tended to be used.

These assumptions, I believe, were that:

1. Ulster was synonymous with the six counties of Northern Ireland rather than the nine counties of the province of Ulster;

2. 'The people of Ulster' were the Protestant people;

3. There was a special relationship between God and that section of the population so that duty to God and support for the State were virtually identified in certain contexts.

It seemed to me that as well as being false, *For God and Ulster* was narrowly exclusive of many of my fellow Ulster men and women. Not only that, but even worse, it was in some respects idolatrous in that for many it effectively put Ulster before God or even in place of God.

I love Northern Ireland dearly. I have a warm affection for its Protestant people who are in a very real sense 'my own people'. But that love and affection for and understanding of Protestants does not allow me to so identify with the state and with the Protestant population that I retain a 'them and us' mentality which would distance me from the people of Ireland beyond the border, or those within Northern Ireland who are Roman Catholic in religion or nationalist in political aspiration. Nor does it allow me to care any less for them or respect them any less.

In regard to my own identity I am increasingly aware that I belong to a denomination which, while most of its churches are within the province of Ulster, spans the whole of the island of Ireland. I am an Irish Presbyterian, and largely through the Presbyterian Church in Ireland I relate to the Church Universal.

Far more important than my membership of any institution which gives me identity, I am above all a child of God the Father and a servant of the Lord Jesus Christ, the Saviour of the world and my personal Saviour. That identity totally transcends for me any lesser identities and transforms them.

Pearl Sagar

Pearl Sagar is a community worker of several years standing in her native East Belfast. She is involved in several initiatives, including the East Belfast Festival, local community and economic development agencies and mother and toddler groups. In 1996 she became one of the two representatives of the Women's Coalition at the multi-party talks.

THIS PHRASE, FOR GOD AND ULSTER POSED A dilemma for me over a number of days as I thought about what it meant to me personally. When I first read the phrase in the letter inviting me to contribute, it meant absolutely nothing. It was a phrase I had heard before but never really attached any meaning to. This led me to really think about its meaning. But after a great deal of thought it still means nothing to me.

The only time I can imagine such a phrase being used is if people were going to war, using something like 'For Queen / King and Country'. The only time I can remember *For God and Ulster* being used is when people spoke of the Battle of the Boyne in 1690. It also makes an appearance on a number of paramilitary murals throughout Northern Ireland.

From birth, my identity has been perceived as Protestant. I was told by my parents that historically this meant that my ancestors protested about being governed by the Church of Rome. This was where Protestantism began, and as a result of this protest, we were able to live free from the Church of Rome and in a democratic environment.

I find the subject of Protestantism a difficult one to write about as it is not something generally discussed. I knew I was a Protestant because my parents told me. As well as this, the area I lived in, the school and church I attended, made it clear. It was never something I gave much thought to - I just accepted it.

The strangest thing about Protestantism I have found is that it is not discussed fully. The only time it crops up that I am aware of is in July and August during the walking season when parades are talking place. This is the only culture I grew up with - nothing else.

I remember at the age of twelve or thirteen finding out that there were other Protestant denominations. The only churches I had heard of were the Catholic Church and the church I belonged to - the Church of Ireland. But when I tried to find out more about Congregationalists, Methodists, Presbyterians and others, people thought I was stupid. So I grew up believing that all churches were the same.

I personally identify myself first and foremost as a human being who is also of the Protestant faith and has the right to live in freedom in a peaceful and democratic society. I believe everyone has that right and will continue to believe this with all my heart, and I hope and pray that the day will come when this is a reality rather than a belief or dream.

Martin Smyth

Martin Smyth was educated at Trinity College, Dublin. Ordained in the Presbyterian Church in Ireland in 1972, he served for ten years as minister of Alexandra Presbyterian Church in Belfast. He resigned this post on being elected as Member of Parliament for South Belfast in 1982 following the murder of Rev Robert Bradford, the sitting MP. He is the Ulster Unionist Party spokesman on Health and Foreign Affairs. A former Imperial Grand Master of the Orange Order, he is Grand Master of the Grand Orange Lodge of Ireland.

IS GOD NOT FIRST?

Some have so used *For God and Ulster* that it has become a slogan debased by their evil exploits, while others have devalued it. Yet such misuse should not blind us to the reality it expresses.

The Lord Jesus set the pattern. To God the things that belong to Him, while rendering unto Caesar that which pertains to his domain. The inherent truth springs from the Garden story and is enshrined in both Old and New Testaments. It is such a part of our innate humanity it is found to a greater or lesser extent in all peoples. Thus we have the perverse understanding that in international or tribal conflicts God is evoked on every side.

Our materialistic generation, which denigrates humanity and spiritual perceptions, questions the truth even as it seeks to deny the personal Deity. Well meaning church people and professing Christians have been snared in this dialectical philosophy. In Northern Ireland this has been heightened by the moral revulsion felt when Roman Catholic IRA members or Protestant loyalists claim that they act in the cause of religion rather than politics.

Specifically in Northern Ireland, as in Devon, the slogan finds its roots in the Williamite banner *Pro Religione et Patria*. It can be seen earlier, for good or ill, in Constantine's *In Hoc Signo Vinci* or the perverse traditions of the mediaeval crusades.

It is vital, therefore, that we do not allow corruption to pervert a glorious reality.

It reminds me of my basic duty as a creature made in the "image of God" and a sinner redeemed by the precious blood of His only beloved Son. God must be first in my life. My prior loyalty is to the Crown Rights of Christ Jesus. This is clearly stamped in the commandments where love of God comes before all else. It is seen equally in the concept of tithing what we have and earn to God. Even superficial examination of this subject in the Bible teaches that such tithes are due on all we have, not merely on what is left when the State has exacted its share and bills are paid. God has first call on us.

Secondly comes our country, our community. This might offend some who strut upon the world scene and claim to be internationalists. It does not mean 'our country, right or wrong'. The moral law of God comes first. As the first disciples found: "We must obey God rather than men" (Acts 5.29). In the early church Christians did not join the Roman Legions voluntarily for they were not willing to swear that Caesar was lord. They knew only Jesus as Lord.

Equally, however, they were committed to live out their lives where they were. To have a missionary vision for other nations and miss the mission field at home is a betrayal of Christian truth. As earlier generations were taught, one will never be a missionary abroad if there is not a witness shown at home.

For me, therefore, the slogan is valid. The corruption is an abomination. God first in my life, lived where I am with no narrow horizon.

Roz Stirling

Roz Stirling has been Youth Officer with the Presbyterian Church in Ireland since 1992. Before that she worked for Universities and Colleges Christian Fellowship in the North East of England and the YMCA in Belfast, having started out as a teacher in Larne. She is a member of the ECONI Steering Group.

IN ULSTER WE HAVE FOR MANY YEARS LIVED WITH slogans. Both communities express something of their identity, roots, fears, hopes and aspirations through them. Slogans are also used as a means of protest to highlight the plight of a community or draw attention to political aspirations.

For God and Ulster is a well known Ulster slogan that draws from me a number of questions and reflections.

It is a slogan that concerns me as one must ask the question, Is allegiance to God being placed on an equal footing with allegiance to Ulster? If individuals or a community embrace the phrase as an expression of their identity are they saying that to be committed to God one must also be committed to Ulster? Are they saying that to be committed to Ulster one must also be committed to God? Or are they claiming that God's honour is somehow tied up with one's being for Ulster - presumably a Protestant Ulster?

As an evangelical Christian seeking to take my personal code of conduct and principles for living from Scripture I have great difficulty with any expression or slogan that even suggests that allegiance to God is equal with any other allegiance. Whether this was the original intention behind the slogan or not, it has the possibility of being interpreted in such a way. The Scriptures make it very clear that God will bless and honour those who love Him firstly and foremostly. The second great commandment - to love our neighbour as ourselves - follows immediately on from this.

To love my neighbour as myself means loving anyone in my sphere of reference, not just those who come from 'my tribe'. Jesus, in fact, makes it very clear that my neighbour is often someone who comes from a different culture, tradition or religious background. The parable of the Good Samaritan was His response to the question "Who is my neighbour?" If I am to love God first and then my neighbour I cannot claim my country to be my second loyalty; my second loyalty must be my neighbour. Moreover, the Bible makes it clear that our citizenship is to be viewed in heavenly terms.

I suspect that for many *For God and Ulster* is about protecting Ulster's Protestant heritage. If this in turn is about protecting the freedom to proclaim the full gospel of Jesus Christ and the full counsel of God as presented in the whole of Scripture then I applaud it, as I applaud anything that ensures the freedom of the gospel. However, in recent days Ulster has seen much activity that is a denial of the gospel and its call to love God and then our neighbour. Jesus went to extreme lengths to relate to those from other cultures. A classic example is His walk through Samaria where He purposefully encountered the woman at the well. Here He crossed four boundaries - political, religious, historical and gender. He crossed these boundaries in order to relate to His neighbour and through that relationship to bring her the words of life. That encounter resulted in her whole community being reached.

When citizens of Ulster, whatever their political allegiance, have courage enough to follow the example of the King of kings and put Him first then God will truly be honoured in Ulster.

Steve Stockman

Steve Stockman was ordained in the Presbyterian Church in Ireland in 1988 and served as assistant minister in 1st Antrim Presbyterian Church. In 1991 he was appointed Youth Development Officer. Since 1994 he has been Dean of Residence at Derryvolgie Hall in Belfast. He is a member of the ECONI Steering Group.

THE ORDER AND CONTEXT OF OUR WORDS - particularly random words in an order almost carved in Sinai stone - can change the meaning of these words. I love God. I reverence Him as an awesome Lord and intimate friend. Ulster is a province of the island where I was born and have lived all my life - a place I love.

Yet appearing together in the phrase *For God and Ulster* gives these words a different hue. Ulster isn't Ulster but just six counties of it. This God is far removed from my God, though those who proclaim it say He is the same biblical God I worship.

Then my confusion about these words and their perversion changes to a deep anger, even rage. *For* and *and,* and the context in which these words are screamed, smash two things I love to pieces with the rocks of prejudice, arrogance, pride and conflict. These words are the antithesis of what my God is about and of the attitude He has to all who are placed in that corner of His world called Ulster.

My anger has been raised to new levels over the summer of 1996 as I have seen the outworking of the phrase. I have watched men in clerical collars and those bearing images of the Bible and scriptural verses on sashes and banners involved side by side with those using violence and the threat of violence. I have no doubt that I have seen evil masquerading behind words that have no root or vine or fruit.

The Bible is about relationships. The vertical relationship with God led Him humbly to give up His rights and sacrificially give His all for those estranged from Him. He was under no obligation to His enemies, but He did it from love. That love transforms those touched by Him so that they might be His body on earth to touch others the same way.

The Bible is about learning to work love into human relationships - a radical love requiring struggle, change, repentance, sacrifice, suffering and death; things experienced, not for our own rights or ends, but for those whom the Bible calls our neighbours and, more radically, our enemies. Following Jesus Christ is about building relationships both within His body and outside it, in order to bring His Kingdom and His will on earth as it is in heaven.

The Bible teaches us how this can be done in the power of God's Holy Spirit. Blessed are the meek, the meek! Blessed are the peacemakers, the peacemakers! Make every effort to live at peace with all men, all men! Love your neighbour as yourself, love your neighbour! Love your enemies, your enemies! That is the revolutionary heart of a gospel that can bring the Kingdom to my home country. Jesus would hardly ask us to pray for it if it were an impossible dream to be given up on.

For God and Ulster should mean reaching out, standing down, apologising and compromising on things that are not matters of biblical principle. It should be about making peace and not offending. It should be the antithesis of Drumcree, Lower Ormeau and wherever else.

Anything else is to take His name in vain; to have other gods before Him. Yet there can be no idols, graven images or challenges to a jealous God who deserves our complete, untainted and unrivalled worship. To put something alongside Him is a dangerous thing. Those who hold this slogan dear would no doubt say that God comes first before Ulster. The words of Jesus would say that by their fruits you shall know them.

Mervyn Storey

Mervyn Storey lives and works in Ballymoney. A member of Ballymoney Free Presbyterian Church, he is a Sunday School teacher, children's worker and lay preacher for the denomination. He is Chairman of the Ballymoney Branch of the Democratic Unionist Party. A member of the Independent Loyal Orange Institution, he is Deputy Master of ILOL 34, District Master of Rasharkin District Lodge ILOL 3, Deputy County Grand Chaplain of the County Grand Lodge of Antrim and Deputy Imperial Grand Chaplain of the Imperial Grand Lodge of Ireland. He is currently Convenor of the Religious Affairs Committee of the Institution. He is also a member of the Apprentice Boys of Derry Finvoy Club and a member of the Knights of Malta.

THIS PHRASE, IN ITS TWO PARTS GIVES US A concise summary of man's duty both to God and to country. It places them in their proper order and puts each in perspective.

For God

This ought to be the aim and desire for man. Our life ought to glorify God. This we do when inwardly we have the highest estimation of God, the greatest confidence in Him and the strongest affection for Him: "Glorify God in your spirit," says Paul (1 Corinthians 6.20). We glorify God, too, when outwardly we acknowledge Him according to His self-revelation - in creation and in Scripture - and when we sincerely endeavour to exalt His name, promote His Kingdom and worship and obey Him according to Scripture.

Yet none of this is possible apart from the grace of God in salvation. Man's heart seeks his own glory - not God's. Yet when God reaches a sinful soul and creates a new heart, He grants new desires and new affections. Only a person who has trusted in the finished work of Christ and has been cleansed by the blood of Christ and who is depending alone on the merit of Christ can truly say *For God.*

This part of the phrase allows nothing alongside God. Unlike the Church of Rome which has God and tradition on an equal footing, it must forever be for God and Him alone.

For Ulster

Why was it necessary to include this second phrase? I believe it is because man not only has a duty towards God but a duty towards his fellow men. If our relationship with God means putting Him first then that will have a bearing on our attitude and actions as citizens of the country in which we live.

The child of God has a responsibility to be a good citizen and to "render unto Caesar that which is Caesar's." Yet if "the powers that be" step into the realm of religion, nothing can be allowed to overrule our responsibility to comply with the dictates of the Almighty. The order of the phrase *For God and Ulster* must ever be kept in the forefront of our minds or, as Scripture puts it, "Seek ye first the Kingdom of God..." (Matthew 6.33).

No public edict should coerce the individual's conscience. In Babylon King Nebuchadnezzar's edict commanding worship of the golden image went unheeded by Shadrach, Meshach and Abednego. Likewise, Daniel resisted the reigning power when "he kneeled upon his knees three times a day, and prayed, and gave thanks before his God, as he did aforetime" (Daniel 6.10).

In Jerusalem Peter and John did not obey the Jewish Council when commanded to speak no more in the name of Jesus. "Whether it be right in the sight of God to hearken unto you more than God, judge ye..." (Acts 4.19), was their response.

Twice in our nation's history under Stuart sovereigns Christian citizens refused to have their consciences coerced and asserted their right of resistance to corrupt powers. The Scottish covenanters resisted the constituted powers when all reasonable and peaceful means had failed to obtain God-given rights and the redress of wrong. The Protestant martyrs resisted the coercion of their consciences by the state and gave their lives rather than defile those consciences. They counted life sweet and death bitter; yet knowing that eternal life was more sweet and eternal death more bitter, they maintained the right to read, believe and obey the Scriptures according to the individual conscience.

In short, the phrase *For God and Ulster* is for me a simple summary of my duty - first to my God, then to my country. Therefore, it is a phrase with which I am quite content.

William Temple

William Temple lived for 28 years in the

Bogside. Now resident in the Fountain

he is actively involved in the community

through the Wapping Community

Association, the Fountain Area

Partnership and the Diamond Project

Trust. He is also involved in cross

community work through the

Northlands Centre and Templegrove

Action Research and as a member of

the advisory committee of the local

Peace and Reconciliation Group. A

member of the Ulster Unionist Party he

is Past President of City and Foyle

Unionist Association. He is a Past

President of the Murray Club,

Apprentice Boys of Derry and Past

Master of No 1 District, City of

Londonderry Royal Arch Purple Chapter.

THE PHRASE *FOR GOD AND ULSTER* AS associated with Loyalist organisations affirms a belief in God and love of Fatherland.

Most loyalist institutions have an initiation ceremony based on the Guild and later Club method which is of English tradition. Before the Reformation members of these Guilds swore upon the relics of a patron saint to be faithful to each other and obey the ruling of the master and wardens. After the Reformation, Protestants dedicated their clubs or institutions to the Glory of God and in memory of a person or persons raised by God to "put a new song into our mouths." However, understanding God's relevance to the loyalist is best explained in the rites practised by some of the early Scottish community in Ulster, rites which were later incorporated into the Orange ritual. The rites illuminate God's control of the universe and emphasise the centrality of God's revealed will to man, as contained in the Holy Bible, for faith and practice.

Ulster to the loyalist is a nine county province of Ireland, six counties in one jurisdiction and three in another. Seven of the nine counties were planted in the early seventeenth century by privileged English and Scottish noblemen and soldiers, who came over with retainers. The majority were Episcopalian - although it is interesting to note that the most densely populated and successful area of the plantation was that of five proportions granted to the Roman Catholic Hamilton family from Scotland. They brought over numerous Catholics and priests, causing the then Episcopalian Bishop of Derry to protest to Parliament regarding the number of Catholics being settled between Strabane and Omagh.

Coincidental with the early years of the plantation, religious persecution was rife in Europe and this brought many to the new developments in search of religious freedom. These refugees were English Quakers and Congregationalists, Scottish Presbyterians and French Huguenots, strong in faith and resolve. They soon outnumbered the planted Protestants and destined a natural tendency that was to effect an Ulster different in composition to the other provinces of Ireland.

The descendants of the religious refugees having only obtained total religious freedom in the nineteenth century feared a reversal of status should Ireland gain Home Rule and became ardent unionists. By the late nineteenth century British culture was predominant within the entire Ulster Protestant community. Coupled with the economic advantages that followed as a consequence of an expanding Empire, this confirmed and ratified the political affiliation with Great Britain.

Today, Ulster Protestants, whether in the six county or three county political arrangement, share the same sentiment about *God and Ulster* - a phrase which adequately expresses a true identity and allegiance.

Chris Walpole

Chris Walpole was born in Dublin and raised in Warrenpoint. He was converted at the age of 16. A businessman for a number of years he became a Candidate for the Methodist Ministry in 1956. Completing his theological training at Edgehill College in Belfast in 1961, he was ordained at the Cork Conference the following year. Since then he has ministered in Methodist churches North and South, and is currently Superintendent of the Upper Erne Circuit in County Fermanagh. He was President of the Methodist Church in Ireland 1995-1996.

THESE WORDS - *FOR GOD AND ULSTER* - ARE familiar to everyone living in Northern Ireland today. They immediately convey to the mind the two things which motivate much of the lives of the people of this province - religion and politics.

For Ulster

The very term 'Ulster' has a political nuance of its own. Here we are dealing with territory and tribal loyalties - the stuff of politics and politicians. What do we mean by this term? Some would wish to see Ulster brought into the confines of a united Ireland, the nationalist aspiration. Others strenuously resist the very thought and are prepared to defend their position. Herein lies the basis for much of the antagonism, misunderstanding, suspicion and fear that we find around us.

For God

Here we try to shake out or disentangle the areas of politics and religion - strands which are so intertwined in Ireland. Here we are challenged to get our priorities right. Jesus was once challenged about his allegiance to the state and to God. His answer was "to render unto Caesar the things that are Caesar's and unto God the things that are God's." Here we must focus, not just upon religion, but upon the Christian religion - upon a God who is revealed to us in Jesus. Through our Lord Jesus

Christ we are challenged to give our first allegiance to God. He is bigger than any religious movement or political party. I believe that if we get the 'God relationship' right other relationships fall into their proper place. Is there a better way in which to express identity? Growing up in the Christian Endeavour movement we often sang 'Ireland for Christ'. That should be our aim. God desires one people who love and serve Him.

Stephen Williams

Stephen Williams was born, raised and educated in Wales. He studied Modern History at Oxford, Theology at Cambridge and completed doctoral study at Yale in 1980. He was ordained as a minister of the Presbyterian Church in Wales in 1980 and appointed to the Chair of Theology at the denominational theological college in Aberystwyth. From 1991-1994 he was based at a theological research institute in Oxford before taking up his present appointment as Professor of Systematic Theology at Union Theological College, Belfast. He is a member of the ECONI Steering Group.

I WRITE AS AN 'OUTSIDER', ONE WHO HAS NOT endured the pain of life in Ulster over the last quarter of a century. And I write without attempting to interpret the historical meaning of *For God and Ulster* or its connotations for the 'insider'.

The coupling of God and... anything - land, cause or person - is perilous. Of course, it has its place. "For the Lord and for Gideon" shouted the Israelites (Judges 7.18). My compatriots rightly seek to act for God and Wales. But these examples also signal warnings. The land of Israel had a unique place in God's purposes in Old Testament times. Even then, territorial acquisition was not an end in itself; it was for the sake of displaying divine righteousness by an obedient pattern of life.

The connection between witness to God and the governance of specific territory is broken in the New Testament. So in any talk, for instance, of *For God and Ulster* I expect every Christian to substitute the name of his or her land for Ulster. More: without adopting any particular political positions, we are to be *For God and Britain, For God and Europe* because we are *For God and the World*. Hence, we identify the glory of God with the confession of His lordship everywhere, and not with one land in particular.

Questions of justice and political settlement necessarily require resolution. No student of the Bible can deny that God is glorified in the quest for and attainment of justice. But the quest must be regulated by at least two principles. First, we must seek peace, which means preparedness to suffer injustice (1 Peter 2.12-25). *For God and Ulster* must be rejected if we can not square it with the proper socio-political application of 1 Peter. Secondly, even if the quest for just order is thwarted, by the grace of justification in Christ, I may still worship in spirit and in truth. Politically securing Ulster for Protestant unionism or loyalism does not necessarily mean gaining the ability to worship in spirit and in truth: in fact, we may, *en route*, destroy spirit and forfeit truth.

One hears folk speak of 'dangerous memories'; if such there be, they are the product of 'dangerous forgetfulness' - forgetfulness of the era of the gospel and the nature of the Lordship of Christ, the suffering servant King. Whether or not political justice favours a form of Union, authentic Christianity demands the primacy of love. Whatever the relation of justice and love, my identity is given, not by a political order, but in union with a crucified Saviour; and as I indwell Christ by faith, so I must indwell my neighbours by love (Luther). Only in subjection to this law of Christ can I even begin to ask about what it might mean to be for Ulster.

Chris Wright

Born in Belfast, Chris Wright began his career as a teacher in Grosvenor High School in 1969. Following completion of a doctorate in Old Testament economic ethics, he was ordained in the Church of England in 1977 serving a curacy in St Peter & St Paul, Tonbridge, Kent. In 1983 he went to India where he taught at the Union Biblical Seminary, Pune. In 1988 he returned to the UK as Director of Studies at All Nations Christian College and was appointed Principal in 1993. He has written several books including Living as the People of God (IVP, 1983), God's People in God's Land (Paternoster, 1990) and Walking in the Ways of the Lord (Apollos, 1995). He has a particular desire to bring to life the relevance of the Old Testament to Christian mission and ethics.

I REMEMBER THIS PHRASE, FOR GOD AND ULSTER, from the banners carried in the Orange parades I watched as a child. Even then this phrase - and the colourful symbols merging Bible and cross with swords, red hands, human kings and rampant horses - seemed somehow incongruous. Now, I consider some of its implied meaning idolatrous.

Without hesitation I thank God for Ulster. It bred in me a love for the Bible, an intelligent evangelical identity and a missionary zeal that defines my maturity. I owe these things also to godly missionary parents, especially my father, Joe Wright - but Ulster made him what he was. At Berry Street Church solid teaching turned my blood biblical. Crusader classes and the Boys' Brigade filled my youth with rich and wholesome memories. My gratitude to God for Ulster is as deep as my love for the place and for my people there.

But *For God and Ulster* summons us to identify our loyalty to God with loyalty, not merely to an earthly country, but to the identity and cause of one particular community within that country. It assumes that God and a form of Ulster Protestantism are so bound together that they will stand or fall together. Let God defend Protestants and advance their cause and Protestants will defend God and advance what they think is His. Loyalty must be to both or you are accused of disloyalty to both.

This attitude is spiritually dangerous - reinforcing cultural pride with impregnable religious certainty; theologically naive - failing to distinguish between the sovereign righteousness of God and the never-more-than-partial rightness of any human cause; and biblically myopic - losing sight of the prophets' challenge to and correction of the people of God in the name of God.

I share my fellow Ulster Protestants' heritage and faith. This tradition has shaped my own cultural roots and identity. But I am ashamed of some aspects of that politico-religious culture - some are the legacy of massive and unrepented historical injustice, some are so suffused with demonic hatred that to say it is for God I consider blasphemous.

It is not only my experience of 'exile' that contributes to a more critical reflection on what the phrase represents - though that has helped. I never was happy with Union Jacks on Belfast churches, any more than I like regimental flags in English churches. Confusion of loyalties to God and state is just too easy, too endemic in human history and too tragically dangerous.

It is not that I want to 'keep God out of politics'. On the contrary, the political arena must be addressed and confronted with the biblical gospel and the stark challenge of the Kingdom of God to all the kingdoms of this world. But that's the point - the gospel confronts the whole political sphere with its ambiguities and differing sides. But those who so totally identify their political cause with the gospel itself are open to no challenge, no critique, no word of correction - not even from the Lord God. Thus, there is no room for repentance, grace, reconciliation. Who needs such things when you know beyond question that God is on your side?

I would replace the phrase on the banners with 'May God have Mercy on Ulster'. That is how I prayed, with tears, as I watched the collapse of the Berlin wall and of South African apartheid. Why not in Ulster too, Lord?

God's mercy is the only hope, but only for those who know they need it. And in the light of the Twelfth 1996: "How long, O Lord, how long?"

Other Publications from ECONI

For God and His Glory Alone

This booklet addresses the key issue of how the Bible can shape and inform our thinking and acting in Northern Ireland. Outlining ten biblical principles relevant to Christian life in our society, the booklet lists passages and questions for further reading, discussion and prayer. Commended by 200 evangelical Christian men and women, the booklet can be used for both personal reflection and group Bible study.
Published 1988   Reprinted 1989   Reprinted 1994   24 pages   Price £1

What Does the Lord Require of us?

In 1992 ECONI launched its Action Pack series. At that launch six talks were given, each of which raised a question of relevance to our community from a biblical perspective. This booklet brings together the text of those talks.
ISBN 1874324 65 4   Published 1993   32 pages   Price £1

A Future With Hope

In 1995 ECONI made a submission to the Forum for Peace and Reconciliation in Dublin. This booklet contains the text of that submission. Following an introduction which assesses the role of religion in the conflict in Northern Ireland, the booklet develops a series of biblical frameworks for peace and reconciliation. This booklet also includes a study guide.
ISBN 1874324 90 5   Published 1995   36 pages   Price £2

Pathways

This is what the Lord says: "Stand at the crossroads and look; ask for the ancient paths, ask where the good way is, and walk in it, and you will find rest for your souls." Jeremiah 6. 16

The conflict in Northern Ireland raises many difficult, sometimes controversial, issues for Christians. Often we choose to ignore or avoid them. Pathways is an attempt to address them biblically. Our goal is to find God's path, *the good way*, and to walk in it.

Beyond Fear, Suspicion and Hostility Alwyn Thomson

How should evangelicals relate to Roman Catholics? This booklet outlines some of the answers to that question coming from evangelicals in Northern Ireland.
ISBN 1874324 75 1   Published 1994   36 pages   Price £2

The Fracture Family Alwyn Thomson

This booklet looks at 'fundamentalism' and 'evangelicalism' in Northern Ireland, challenges some of the assumptions often made about them and explains the evanglical foundations of ECONI.
ISBN 1874324 85 9   Published 1995   36 pages   Price £2

A NUMBER OF OTHER PATHWAYS TITLES ARE PLANNED

Action Packs

ECONI Action Packs develop the principles raised in *For God and His Glory Alone*. Each pack focuses on one of the ten biblical themes and includes a detailed Bible study, discussion material for youth groups, house groups and leadership groups, resource materials - worksheets, drama scripts, OHP illustrations and action lists.

Ten packs are available

- Citizenship
- Forgiveness
- Hope
- Justice & Righteousness
- Love
- Peace
- Reconciliation
- Repentance
- Servanthood
- Truth

Packs can be purchased separately for £2.50 or as a set of ten in a binder for £20.00.

Public Statements

The work of ECONI has many aspects. As one part of this work ECONI has, over the past number of years, spoken out publicly on a number of critical developments in the life of our community. Among these are:

A Statement of Concern
Response to the Downing Street Declaration 17 December 1993

God's Call to Peacemaking
An evangelical response to the IRA ceasefire 7 September 1994

Building Hope
An evangelical response to the Loyalist ceasefire 21 October 1994

A Future with Hope
Verbal submission to the Forum for Peace and Reconciliation 12 April 1995

A Time to Listen
An evangelical response to the ending of the IRA ceasefire 16 February 1996

These statements have been gathered together and published in a 16 page pamphlet, Public Statements, *available for fifty pence.*

Information

If you would like to order any of our publications or would like to know more
about the work of ECONI please contact us at:

ECONI
12 Wellington Place
BELFAST BT1 6GE
Telephone: (01232) 325258 Fax:(01232) 434156
Email: admin@econi.dnet.co.uk